Bringing Up GODLY GIRLS

365 Daily Devotions for Parents

Freeman-Smith, a division of Worthy Media, Inc.
134 Franklin Road, Suite 200, Brentwood, Tennessee 37027

The quoted ideas expressed in this book (but not Scripture verses) are not, in all cases, exact quotations, as some have been edited for clarity and brevity. In all cases, the author has attempted to maintain the speaker's original intent. In some cases, quoted material for this book was obtained from secondary sources, primarily print media. While every effort was made to ensure the accuracy of these sources, the accuracy cannot be guaranteed. For additions, deletions, corrections, or clarifications in future editions of this text, please write Freeman-Smith.

Cover Design by Kim Russell / Wahoo Designs
Page Layout by Bart Dawson

ISBN 978-1-60587-337-4

Printed in the United States of America

Bringing Up GODLY GIRLS

365 Daily Devotions for Parents

A MESSAGE TO PARENTS

In your hands, you hold a 365-day devotional book that focuses on you and your daughter. Congratulations—your willingness to add a new tool to your parenting toolkit shows that you're determined to raise a responsible young woman.

During the next year, you'll be asked to read, to study, to learn, and to talk to your daughter every day. Discuss with her the talking points and the quotes with the heading of "A Quote to Talk About" and ask what that quote means to her. Also, take time to reflect on the parent tips. When you do these things, you will become a better parent and your girl will become a better person.

So, read these devotionals carefully and take the ideas on these pages to heart. When you do, you'll learn that it's not always easy to raise a godly girl, but it's always worth the effort. And, you'll learn that there's absolutely no challenge—not even the critically important challenge of caring for your daughter—that you and God, working together, can't handle.

RAISING A GODLY DAUGHTER

Train up a child in the way he should go, and when he is old he will not depart from it.

PROVERBS 22:6 NKJV

If your daughter is like most young women, she will seek the admiration of her friends and classmates. But the eagerness to please others should never overshadow her eagerness to please God. God has big plans for your daughter, and if your child intends to fulfill God's plans by following God's Son, then your daughter must seek to please the Father first and always.

Do you want your child to be successful and happy? Then encourage her to study God's Word and live by it. If your daughter follows that advice, then when she faces a difficult choice or a powerful temptation, she'll be prepared to meet the enemy head-on.

So, as a parent, your task is straightforward: encourage your child to seek God's approval in every aspect of her life. Does this sound too simple? Perhaps it is simple, but it is also the only way for your daughter to reap the marvelous riches that God has in store for her.

A Talking Point

Today, talk to your daughter about the dangers of immorality and the rewards of obedience.

Day 2

BEHAVING RESPONSIBLY

For the hearers of the law are not righteous before God, but the doers of the law will be declared righteous.

ROMANS 2:13 HCSB

How hard is it for young people to act responsibly? Sometimes, when youngsters are beset by negative role models and relenting peer pressure, it can be very difficult for them to do the right thing. Difficult, but not impossible.

Nobody needs to tell your daughter the obvious: She has many responsibilities—obligations to herself, to her family, to her community, to her school, and to her Creator. And which of these duties should take priority? The answer can be found in Matthew 6:33: "But seek first the kingdom of God and His righteousness, and all these things will be provided for you" (HCSB).

When your daughter learns the importance of honoring God with her time, her talents, and her prayers, she'll be much more likely to behave responsibly. So encourage your daughter to take all her duties seriously, especially her duties to God. If she follows your advice, your child will soon discover that pleasing God isn't just the right thing to do; it's also the best way to live.

A Talking Point

Today, talk to your daughter about the rewards of behaving responsibly.

A LOVE THAT CHANGES EVERYTHING

Your old life is dead. Your new life, which is your real life—even though invisible to spectators—is with Christ in God. He is your life.

COLOSSIANS 3:3 MSG

What does the love of Christ mean to His believers? It changes everything. His love is perfect and steadfast. Even though we are fallible, and wayward, the Good Shepherd cares for us still. Even though we have fallen far short of the Father's commandments, Christ loves us with a power and depth that is beyond our understanding. And, as we accept Christ's love and walk in Christ's footsteps, our lives bear testimony to His power and to His grace. Yes, Christ's love changes everything; may we invite Him into our hearts so it can then change everything in us.

A Parent Tip

Through His sacrifice on the cross, Jesus demonstrated His love for you and your child. As a responsible parent, it's up to you to make certain your youngster understands that Christ's love changes everything.

Day 4

THE NEED TO BE DISCIPLINED

Do you not know that those who run in a race all run, but only one receives the prize? Run in such a way that you may win. Everyone who competes in the games exercises self-control in all things.

1 CORINTHIANS 9:24-25 NASB

God is clear: we must exercise self-discipline in all matters. Self-discipline is not simply a proven way to get ahead, it's also an integral part of God's plan for our lives. If we genuinely seek to be faithful stewards of our time, our talents, and our resources, we must adopt a disciplined approach to life. Otherwise, our talents are wasted and our resources are squandered.

Our greatest rewards result from hard work and perseverance. May we, as disciplined believers, be willing to work for the rewards we so earnestly desire.

A Parent Tip

Be disciplined in your own approach to life. You can't teach it if you won't live it.

Day 5

CELEBRATING OTHERS

So encourage each other and give each other strength, just as you are doing now.

1 THESSALONIANS 5:11 NCV

Do you delight in the victories of others? You should. Each day provides countless opportunities to encourage your loved ones and to praise their good works. When you do so, you not only spread seeds of joy and happiness, you also obey the commandments of God's Holy Word.

As Christians, we are called upon to spread the Good News of Christ, and we are also called to spread a message of encouragement and hope to our families and to the world. So, let us be cheerful Christian parents with smiles on our faces and encouraging words on our lips. By blessing others, we also bless ourselves, and, at the same time, we do honor to the One who gave His life for us.

A Parent Tip

Today, make a special effort to celebrate your daughter's accomplishments.

Day 6

THE IMPORTANCE OF PRAYER

Be anxious for nothing, but in everything by prayer and supplication, with thanksgiving, let your requests be made known to God.

PHILIPPIANS 4:6 NKJV

Prayer is a powerful tool for communicating with our Creator; it is an opportunity to commune with the Giver of all things good. Prayer is not a thing to be taken lightly or to be used infrequently. Prayer should never be reserved for mealtimes or for bedtimes; it should be an ever-present focus in our daily lives.

In his first letter to the Thessalonians, Paul wrote, "Rejoice evermore. Pray without ceasing. In every thing give thanks: for this is the will of God in Christ Jesus concerning you" (5:17-18 KJV). Paul's words apply to every Christian of every generation. So, let us pray constantly about things great and small. God is listening, and He wants to hear from us. Now.

A Parent Tip

Don't ever be embarrassed to pray: Are you embarrassed to bow your head in a restaurant? Don't be; it's the people who aren't praying who should be embarrassed!

THE POWER OF FAITH

Have faith in the Lord your God, and you will stand strong. Have faith in his prophets, and you will succeed.

2 CHRONICLES 20:20 NCV

Every life—including yours—is a series of successes and failures, celebrations and disappointments, joys and sorrows. Every step of the way, through every triumph and tragedy, God will stand by your side and strengthen you . . . if you have faith in Him. Jesus taught His disciples that if they had faith, they could move mountains. You can too.

When you place your faith, your trust, indeed your life in the hands of Christ Jesus, you'll be amazed at the marvelous things He can do with you and through you. So strengthen your faith through praise, through worship, through Bible study, and through prayer. And trust God's plans. With Him, all things are possible, and He stands ready to open a world of possibilities to you . . . if you have faith.

A Quote to Talk About

Faith is an act of the will, a choice, based on the unbreakable Word of a God who cannot lie, and who showed what love and obedience and sacrifice mean, in the person of Jesus Christ.

ELISABETH ELLIOT

Day 8

NEW BEGINNINGS

Do not remember the former things, nor consider the things of old. Behold, I will do a new thing.

ISAIAH 43:18-19 NKJV

Each new day offers countless opportunities to serve God, to seek His will, and to obey His teachings. But each day also offers countless opportunities to stray from God's commandments and to wander far from His path.

Sometimes, we wander aimlessly in a wilderness of our own making, but God has better plans for us. And, whenever we ask Him to renew our strength and guide our steps, He does so.

Consider this day a new beginning. Consider it a fresh start, a renewed opportunity to serve your Creator with willing hands and a loving heart. Ask God to renew your sense of purpose as He guides your steps. Today is a glorious opportunity to serve your Father in heaven. Seize that opportunity while you can; tomorrow may indeed be too late.

A Talking Point

Today, talk to your daughter about the wonderful opportunities that God has in store for her.

Day 9

YOUR DAUGHTER'S SELF-IMAGE

God is love, and the one who remains in love remains in God, and God remains in him.

1 JOHN 4:16 HCSB

While there are many factors that will have an impact on your daughter's self-image, three elements are extremely important: 1. a sense of worthiness 2. a sense of belonging 3. a sense of competency.

As a Christian parent, you should help your daughter recognize that she is already worthy (because of God's grace and His love) and that she already belongs to your family and to God's family. What's left, then, is for your daughter to develop a sense of competence, which usually comes from hard work, dedication, and plenty of practice. As a parent, you can encourage your child to do the work that's required to achieve excellence. But you can't force her to become competent—ultimately, she must gain competence for herself.

A Talking Point

Today, remind your daughter that she is beloved by you and by God.

Day 10

THE ULTIMATE INSTRUCTION MANUAL

The one who has contempt for instruction will pay the penalty, but the one who respects a command will be rewarded.

PROVERBS 13:13 HCSB

The Holy Bible contains thorough instructions which, if followed, lead to fulfillment, righteousness, and salvation. But, if we choose to ignore God's commandments, the results are as predictable as they are tragic.

A righteous life has many components: faith, honesty, generosity, love, kindness, humility, gratitude, and worship, to name but a few. If we seek to follow the steps of our Savior, Jesus Christ, we must seek to live according to His commandments. Let us follow God's commandments, and let us conduct our lives in such a way that we might be shining examples for those who have not yet found Christ.

A Quote to Talk About

To yield to God means to belong to God, and to belong to God means to have all His infinite power. To belong to God means to have all.

HANNAH WHITALL SMITH

THE LORD IS NEAR

Come near to God, and God will come near to you. You sinners, clean sin out of your lives. You who are trying to follow God and the world at the same time, make your thinking pure.

JAMES 4:8 NCV

Since God is everywhere, we are free to sense His presence whenever we take the time to quiet our souls and turn our prayers to Him. But sometimes, amid the incessant demands of everyday life, we turn our thoughts far from God; when we do, we suffer.

Do you set aside quiet moments each day to offer praise to your Creator? As a parent who has received the gift of God's grace, you most certainly should. Silence is a gift that you give to yourself and to God.

The familiar words of Psalm 46:10 remind us to "Be still, and know that I am God." When we do so, we encounter the awesome presence of our loving Heavenly Father, and we are comforted in the knowledge that God is not just near. He is here.

A Quote to Talk About

God walks with us. He scoops us up in His arms or simply sits with us in silent strength until we cannot avoid the awesome recognition that yes, even now, He is here.

GLORIA GAITHER

Day 12

SEEKING HIS WILL

Teach me to do Your will, for You are my God; Your Spirit is good. Lead me in the land of uprightness.

PSALM 143:10 NKJV

God has a plan for our world and our lives. God does not do things by accident; He is willful and intentional. Unfortunately for us, we cannot always understand the will of God. Why? Because we are mortal beings with limited understanding. Although we cannot fully comprehend the will of God, we should always trust the will of God.

As this day unfolds, seek God's will and obey His Word. When you entrust your life to Him without reservation, He will give you the courage to meet any challenge, the strength to endure any trial, and the wisdom to live in His righteousness and in His peace.

A Talking Point

Today, talk to your daughter about God's will, and remind her that God's plans are always best.

Day 13

GOOD HABITS, BAD HABITS

Do not be fooled: "Bad friends will ruin good habits."

1 CORINTHIANS 15:33 NCV

It's an old saying and a true one: First, you make your habits, and then your habits make you. Some habits will inevitably bring you closer to God; other habits will lead you away from the path He has chosen for you. If you sincerely desire to improve your spiritual health, you must honestly examine the habits that make up the fabric of your day. And you must abandon those habits that are displeasing to God.

If you trust God, and if you keep asking for His help, He can transform your life. If you sincerely ask Him to help you, the same God who created the universe will help you defeat the harmful habits that have heretofore defeated you. So, if at first you don't succeed, keep praying. God is listening, and He's ready to help you become a better person if you ask Him . . . so ask today.

A Talking Point

Today, talk to your daughter about the need to establish healthy habits.

Day 14

CHOOSING THE GOOD LIFE

And in that day you will ask Me nothing. Most assuredly, I say to you, whatever you ask the Father in My name He will give you. Until now you have asked nothing in My name. Ask, and you will receive, that your joy may be full.

JOHN 16:23-24 NKJV

God offers us abundance through His Son, Jesus. When we entrust our hearts and our days to the One who created us, we experience abundance through the grace and sacrifice of His Son, Jesus. But, when we turn our thoughts and our energies away from God's commandments, we inevitably forfeit the spiritual abundance that might otherwise be ours.

What is your focus today? Are you a parent who is focused on God's Word and His will for your life? Or are you focused on the distractions and temptations of a difficult world. The answer to this question will, to a surprising extent, determine the quality and the direction of your day.

If you sincerely seek the spiritual abundance that your Savior offers, then follow Him completely and without reservation. When you do, you will receive the love, the life, and the abundance that He has promised.

A Talking Point

Today, talk to your daughter about the real meaning of abundance.

TO JUDGE OR NOT TO JUDGE

When they persisted in questioning Him, He stood up and said to them, "The one without sin among you should be the first to throw a stone at her."

JOHN 8:7 HCSB

The warning of Matthew 7:1 is clear: "Judge not, that ye be not judged" (KJV). Yet even the most devoted Christians may fall prey to a powerful yet subtle temptation: the temptation to judge others. But as obedient followers of Christ, we are commanded to refrain from such behavior.

As Jesus came upon a young woman who had been condemned by the Pharisees, He spoke not only to the crowd that was gathered there, but also to all generations when He warned, "He that is without sin among you, let him first cast a stone at her" (John 8:7 KJV). Christ's message is clear, and it applies not only to the Pharisees of ancient times, but also to us.

A Quote to Talk About

Judging draws the judgment of others.

CATHERINE MARSHALL

Day 16

NEVER-ENDING LOVE

And God gave us this command: Those who love God must also love their brothers and sisters.

1 JOHN 4:21 NCV

C. S. Lewis observed, "A man's spiritual health is exactly proportional to his love for God." If we are to enjoy the spiritual health that God intends for us, we must praise Him, we must love Him, and we must obey Him.

When we worship God faithfully and obediently, we invite His love into our hearts. When we truly worship God, we allow Him to rule over our days and our lives. In turn, we grow to love God even more deeply as we sense His love for us.

Today, open your heart to the Father. And let your obedience be a fitting response to His never-ending love.

A Parent Tip

To a child, a parent's unconditional love serves as a representation of every other kind of love, including God's love. So parental love should be demonstrated with deeds, not just announced with words. Thoughtful parents demonstrate their love by giving their kids heaping helpings of time, attention, discipline, protection, and nurturing.

LIVING RIGHTEOUSLY

Run away from infantile indulgence. Run after mature righteousness—faith, love, peace—joining those who are in honest and serious prayer before God.

2 TIMOTHY 2:22 MSG

A life of righteousness is lived in accordance with God's commandments. A righteous believer strives to be faithful, honest, generous, disciplined, loving, kind, humble, and grateful, to name only a few of the more obvious qualities which are described in God's Word.

If we seek to follow the steps of Jesus, we must seek to live according to His teachings. In short, we must, to the best of our abilities, live according to the principles contained in the Holy Bible. When we do, we become powerful examples to our families, to our friends, and to the world.

A Parent Tip

Even well-meaning parents may be tempted to hand over the task of teaching to the "experts" down at the local school. But God's Word is clear: Parents—not teachers or coaches—bear the ultimate responsibility for instructing their youngsters and imparting the essential elements of God's wisdom.

Day 18

GIVE ME PATIENCE . . . NOW!

Rest in the Lord, and wait patiently for Him.

PSALM 37:7 NKJV

Psalm 37:7 commands us to wait patiently for God. But as busy parents in a fast-paced world, many of us find that waiting quietly for God is difficult. Why? Because we are fallible human beings seeking to live according to our own timetables, not God's. In our better moments, we realize that patience is not only a virtue, it is also a commandment from God.

We human beings are impatient by nature. We know what we want, and we know exactly when we want it: NOW! But, God knows better. He has created a world that unfolds according to His plans, not our own. As believers, we must trust His wisdom and His goodness.

God instructs us to be patient in all things. We must be patient with our families, our friends, and our associates. We must also be patient with our Creator as He unfolds His plan for our lives. And that's as it should be. After all, think how patient God has been with us.

A Parent Tip

Every family puts something or someone in first place. Does God occupy first place in your family? If so, congratulations! If not, it's time to reorder your priorities.

MAINTAINING PERSPECTIVE

It is important to look at things from God's point of view.

1 CORINTHIANS 4:6 MSG

If a temporary loss of perspective has left you worried, exhausted, or both, it's time to readjust your thought patterns. Negative thoughts are habit-forming; thankfully, so are positive ones. With practice, you can form the habit of focusing on God's priorities and your possibilities. When you do, you'll soon discover that you will spend less time fretting about your challenges and more time praising God for His gifts.

When you call upon the Lord and prayerfully seek His will, He will give you wisdom and perspective. When you make God's priorities your priorities, He will direct your steps and calm your fears. So today and every day hereafter, pray for a sense of balance and perspective. And remember: no problems are too big for God—and that includes yours.

A Quote to Talk About

The Bible is a remarkable commentary on perspective. Through its divine message, we are brought face to face with issues and tests in daily living and how, by the power of the Holy Spirit, we are enabled to respond positively to them.

LUCI SWINDOLL

Day 20

A LIFE OF ABUNDANCE

I have come that they may have life, and that they may have it more abundantly.

JOHN 10:10 NKJV

What, exactly, did Jesus mean when He promised "life . . . more abundantly"? Was He referring to material possessions or financial wealth? Hardly. Jesus offers a different kind of abundance: a spiritual richness that extends beyond the temporal boundaries of this world.

Is material abundance part of God's plan for our lives? Perhaps. But in every circumstance of life, during times of wealth or times of want, God will provide us what we need if we trust Him. May we, as believers, claim the riches of Christ every day that we live, and may we share His blessings with all who cross our path.

As you organize your day and care for your family, accept God's promise of spiritual abundance . . . you may be certain that when you do your part, God will do His.

A Parent Tip

When Jesus talked about abundance, was He talking about "money"? The answer is no. When Christ talked about abundance, He was concerned with people's spiritual well-being, not their financial well-being. That's a lesson that you must learn . . . and it's a lesson that you must share with your daughter.

IN TIMES OF ADVERSITY

For everyone born of God overcomes the world. This is the victory that has overcome the world, even our faith.

1 JOHN 5:4 NIV

All of us face times of adversity. On occasion, we all must endure the disappointments and tragedies that befall believers and nonbelievers alike. The reassuring words of 1 John 5:4 remind us that when we accept God's grace, we overcome the passing hardships of this world by relying upon His strength, His love, and His promise of eternal life.

When we face the inevitable difficulties of life, God stands ready to protect us. Our responsibility, of course, is to ask Him for protection. When we call upon Him in heartfelt prayer, He will answer—in His own time and according to His own plan—and He will heal us. And while we are waiting for God's plans to unfold and for His healing touch to restore us, we can be comforted in the knowledge that our Creator can overcome any obstacle, even if we cannot. Let us take God at His word, and let us trust Him.

A Talking Point

Today, remind your daughter that tough times are simply opportunities to trust God completely and to find strength in Him.

Day 22

DISCIPLINE YOURSELF

Discipline yourself for the purpose of godliness.

1 TIMOTHY 4:7 NASB

Are you a self-disciplined person and a self-disciplined parent? If so, congratulations . . . your disciplined approach to life can help you build a more meaningful relationship with God. Why? Because God expects all His believers (including you) to lead lives of disciplined obedience to Him . . . and He rewards those believers who do.

Sometimes, it's hard to be dignified and disciplined. Why? Because you live in a world where many prominent people want you to believe that dignified, self-disciplined behavior is going out of style. But don't deceive yourself: self-discipline never goes out of style.

Your greatest accomplishments will probably require plenty of work and a heaping helping of self-discipline—which, by the way, is perfectly fine with God. After all, He knows that you're up to the task, and He has big plans for you. God will do His part to fulfill those plans, and the rest, of course, depends upon you.

A Talking Point

Today, remind your daughter that when she makes wise choices, she also builds self-confidence.

PATS ON THE BACK

So then, we must pursue what promotes peace and what builds up one another.

ROMANS 14:19 HCSB

Life is a team sport, and all of us need occasional pats on the back from our teammates. In the book of Ephesians, Paul writes, "Do not let any unwholesome talk come out of your mouths, but only what is helpful for building others up according to their needs, that it may benefit those who listen" (4:29 NIV). Paul reminds us that when we choose our words carefully, we can have a powerful impact on those around us.

Since we don't always know who needs our help, the best strategy is to encourage all the people who cross our paths. So today, be a world-class source of encouragement to everyone you meet. Never has the need been greater.

A Parent Tip

Make encouragement a habit by deliberately looking for ways to encourage and praise your daughter every day.

Day 24

YOU ARE BLESSED

I will bless them and the places surrounding my hill. I will send down showers in season; there will be showers of blessings.

EZEKIEL 34:26 NIV

If you sat down and began counting your blessings, how long would it take? A very, very long time! Your blessings include life, freedom, family, friends, talents, and possessions, for starters. But, your greatest blessing—a gift that is yours for the asking—is God's gift of salvation through Christ Jesus.

Today, begin making a list of your blessings. You most certainly will not be able to make a complete list, but take a few moments and jot down as many blessings as you can. Then give thanks to the giver of all good things: God. His love for you is eternal, as are His gifts. And it's never too soon—or too late—to offer Him thanks.

A Parent Tip

If you need a little cheering up, start counting your blessings. In truth, you really have too many blessings to count, but it never hurts to try.

Day 25

WHAT DOESN'T CHANGE

Jesus Christ is the same yesterday, today, and forever.

HEBREWS 13:8 NCV

Our world is in a state of constant change. God is not. At times, the world seems to be trembling beneath our feet. But we can be comforted in the knowledge that our Heavenly Father is the rock that cannot be shaken. His Word promises, "I am the Lord, I do not change" (Malachi 3:6 NKJV).

Every day that we live, we mortals encounter a multitude of changes—some good, some not so good, some downright disheartening. On those occasions when we must endure life-changing personal losses that leave us breathless, there is a place we can turn for comfort and assurance—we can turn to God. When we do, our loving Heavenly Father stands ready to protect us, to comfort us, to guide us, and, in time, to heal us.

A Parent Tip

Change is inevitable; growth is not. God will come to your doorstep on countless occasions with opportunities to learn and to grow. And He will knock. Your challenge, of course, is to open the door.

CLAIMING THE JOY

A cheerful heart has a continual feast.

PROVERBS 15:15 HCSB

On some days, as every parent knows, it's hard to be cheerful. Sometimes, as the demands of the world increase and our energy sags, we feel less like "cheering up" and more like "tearing up." But even in our darkest hours, we can turn to God, and He will give us comfort.

Few things in life are more sad, or, for that matter, more absurd, than a grumpy Christian. Christ promises us lives of abundance and joy, but He does not force His joy upon us. We must claim His joy for ourselves, and when we do, Jesus, in turn, fills our spirits with His power and His love.

When we place Jesus at the center of our lives and trust Him as our personal Savior, He will transform us, not just for today, but for all eternity. Then we, as God's children, can share Christ's joy and His message with a world that needs both.

A Talking Point

Remind your daughter that happiness is not a goal. Genuine happiness is the by-product of a right relationship with God.

Day 27

ENTHUSIASTIC SERVICE

Do your work with enthusiasm. Work as if you were serving the Lord, not as if you were serving only men and women.

EPHESIANS 6:7 NCV

Do you see each day as a glorious opportunity to serve God and to do His will? Are you enthused about life, or do you struggle through each day giving scarcely a thought to God's blessings? Are you constantly praising God for His gifts, and are you sharing His Good News with the world? And are you excited about the possibilities for service that God has placed before you, whether at home, at work, at church, or at school? You should be.

You are the recipient of Christ's sacrificial love. Accept it enthusiastically and share it fervently. Jesus deserves your enthusiasm; the world deserves it; and you deserve the experience of sharing it.

A Talking Point

Today, talk to your daughter about the power of enthusiasm.

Day 28

THE MASTER'S TOUCH

Everything is possible to the one who believes.

MARK 9:23 HCSB

When a suffering woman sought healing by simply touching the hem of His garment, Jesus turned and said, "Daughter, be of good comfort; thy faith hath made thee whole" (Matthew 9:22 KJV). We, too, can be made whole when we place our faith completely in the person of Jesus Christ.

Concentration camp survivor Corrie ten Boom relied on faith during her ten months of imprisonment and torture. Later, despite the fact that four of her family members had died in Nazi death camps, Corrie's faith was unshaken. She wrote, "There is no pit so deep that God's love is not deeper still."

If your faith is being tested to the point of breaking, know that your Savior is near. If you reach out to Him in faith, He will give you peace and heal your broken spirit. Be content to touch even the smallest fragment of the Master's garment, and He will make you whole.

A Quote to Talk About

When life is difficult, God wants us to have a faith that trusts and waits.

KAY ARTHUR

BUILDING FELLOWSHIP

Behold, how good and how pleasant it is for brethren to dwell together in unity!

PSALM 133:1 NKJV

Fellowship with other believers should be an integral part of your family's everyday life. Your association with fellow Christians should be uplifting, enlightening, encouraging, and consistent.

Are you an active member of your own fellowship? Are you a builder of bridges inside the four walls of your church and outside it? Do you contribute to God's glory by contributing your time and your talents to a close-knit band of believers? Hopefully so. The fellowship of believers is intended to be a powerful tool for spreading God's Good News and uplifting His children. And God intends for you to be a fully contributing member of that fellowship. Your intentions should be the same.

A Quote to Talk About

In God's economy you will be hard-pressed to find many examples of successful "Lone Rangers."

LUCI SWINDOLL

EXTREME CHANGES

Then He said to them all, "If anyone wants to come with Me, he must deny himself, take up his cross daily, and follow Me."

LUKE 9:23 HCSB

Jesus made an extreme sacrifice for you. Are you willing to make extreme changes in your life for Him? Can you honestly say that you're passionate about your faith and that you're really following Jesus? Hopefully so. But if you're preoccupied with other things—or if you're strictly a one-day-a-week Christian—then you're in need of an extreme spiritual makeover!

Nothing is more important than your wholehearted commitment to your Creator and to His only begotten Son. Your faith must never be an afterthought; it must be your ultimate priority, your ultimate possession, and your ultimate passion. You are the recipient of Christ's love. Accept it enthusiastically and share it passionately. Jesus deserves your extreme enthusiasm; the world deserves it; and you deserve the experience of sharing it.

A Parent Tip

How can you and your daughter guard your steps? By walking with Jesus every day of your life.

Day 31

FRIENDSHIPS THAT HONOR GOD

If your life honors the name of Jesus, he will honor you.

2 THESSALONIANS 1:12 MSG

Some friendships help us honor God; these friendships should be nurtured. Other friendships place us in situations where we are tempted to dishonor God by disobeying His commandments; friendships such as these have the potential to do us great harm.

Because we tend to become like our friends, we must choose our friends carefully. Because our friends influence us in ways that are both subtle and powerful, we must ensure that our friendships are pleasing to God. When we spend our days in the presence of godly believers, we are blessed, not only by those friends, but also by our Creator.

A Talking Point

Today, talk to your daughter about the need to establish friendships with people who fear God and honor Christ.

Day 32

THE MIRACLE WORKER

Jesus said to them, "I have shown you many great miracles from the Father."

JOHN 10:32 NIV

God is a miracle worker. Throughout history He has intervened in the course of human events in ways that cannot be explained by science or human rationale. And He's still doing so today.

God's miracles are not limited to special occasions, nor are they witnessed by a select few. God is crafting His wonders all around us: the miracle of the birth of a new baby; the miracle of a world renewing itself with every sunrise; the miracle of lives transformed by God's love and grace. Each day, God's handiwork is evident for all to see and experience.

Today, seize the opportunity to inspect God's hand at work. His miracles come in a variety of shapes and sizes, so keep your eyes and your heart open. Be watchful, and you'll soon be amazed.

A Quote to Talk About

When we face an impossible situation, all self-reliance and self-confidence must melt away; we must be totally dependent on Him for the resources.

ANNE GRAHAM LOTZ

CHOOSING KINDNESS

Kind people do themselves a favor, but cruel people bring trouble on themselves.

PROVERBS 11:17 NCV

If we believe the words of Proverbs 11:17—and we should—then we understand that kindness is its own reward. And, if we are to obey the commandments of our Savior—and we should—we must sow seeds of kindness wherever we go.

Kindness is a choice. Sometimes, when we feel happy or generous, we find it easy to be kind. Other times, when we are discouraged or tired, we can scarcely summon the energy to utter a single kind word. But, God's commandment is clear: He intends that we make the conscious choice to treat others with kindness and respect, no matter our circumstances, no matter our emotions. Kindness, therefore, is a choice that we, as Christians must make many times each day.

A Parent Tip

Kindness is contagious; kids can catch it from their parents.

Day 34

YOUR SHINING LIGHT

While ye have light, believe in the light, that ye may be the children of light.

JOHN 12:36 KJV

The Bible says that you are "the light that gives light to the world." What kind of light have you been giving off? Hopefully, you've been a good example for everybody to see. Why? Because the world needs all the light it can get, and that includes your light, too!

Christ showed enduring love for you by willingly sacrificing His own life so that you might have eternal life. As a response to His sacrifice, you should love Him, praise Him, and share His message of salvation with your neighbors and with the world. So let your light shine today and every day. When you do, God will bless you now and forever.

A Parent Tip

As a parent, the most important light you will ever shine is the light that your own life shines on the lives of your children. Proclaiming your faith is never enough—you must also demonstrate it.

Day 35

NEW BEGINNINGS

I will give you a new heart and put a new spirit in you….

EZEKIEL 36:26 NIV

If we sincerely want to change ourselves for the better, we must start on the inside and work our way out from there. Lasting change doesn't occur "out there"; it occurs "in here." It occurs, not in the shifting sands of our own particular circumstances, but in the quiet depths of our own hearts.

Are you in search of a new beginning or, for that matter, a new you? If so, don't expect changing circumstances to miraculously transform you into the person you want to become. Transformation starts with God, and it starts in the silent center of a humble human heart—like yours.

A Quote to Talk About

In those desperate times when we feel like we don't have an ounce of strength, He will gently pick up our heads so that our eyes can behold something—something that will keep His hope alive in us.

KATHY TROCCOLI

Day 36

SAYING YES TO GOD

So do not fear, for I am with you; do not be dismayed, for I am your God. I will strengthen you and help you; I will uphold you with my righteous right hand.

ISAIAH 41:10 NIV

Your decision to seek a deeper relationship with God will not remove all problems from your life; to the contrary, it will bring about a series of personal crises as you constantly seek to say "yes" to Him although the world encourages you to do otherwise. Each time you are tempted to distance yourself from God, you will face a spiritual crisis. A few of these crises may be monumental in scope, but most will be the small, everyday decisions of life. In fact, life can be seen as one test after another—and with each crisis comes yet another opportunity to grow closer to God.

Today, you will face many opportunities to say "yes" to your Creator—and you will also encounter many opportunities to say "no" to Him. Your answers will determine the quality of your day and the direction of your life, so answer carefully . . . very carefully.

A Parent Tip

Teach your kids that worship isn't just for Sunday mornings. Demonstrate to your family that worshipping God is a seven-day-a-week proposition, not a one-day-a-week intermission.

PRAISE HIM

Praise the Lord! Oh, give thanks to the Lord, for He is good! For His mercy endures forever.

PSALM 106:1 NKJV

Sometimes, in our rush "to get things done," we simply don't stop long enough to pause and thank our Creator for the countless blessings He has bestowed upon us. But when we slow down and express our gratitude to the One who made us, we enrich our own lives and the lives of those around us.

Thanksgiving should become a habit, a regular part of our daily routines. God has blessed us beyond measure, and we owe Him everything, including our eternal praise. Let us praise Him today, tomorrow, and throughout eternity.

A Parent Tip

You can't count all your blessings, they're simply too many of them. But, as a Christian parent, you know where to start counting: Your Heavenly Father, His only Son, and your own children.

Day 38

TAKING RISKS

Is anything too hard for the Lord?

GENESIS 18:14 NKJV

As we consider the uncertainties of the future, we are confronted with a powerful temptation: the temptation to "play it safe." Unwilling to move mountains, we fret over molehills. Unwilling to entertain great hopes for tomorrow, we focus on the unfairness of today. Unwilling to trust God completely, we take timid half-steps when God intends that we make giant leaps.

Today, ask God for the courage to step beyond the boundaries of your doubts. Ask Him to guide you to a place where you can realize your full potential—a place where you are freed from the fear of failure. Ask Him to do His part, and promise Him that you will do your part. Don't ask Him to lead you to a "safe" place; ask Him to lead you to the "right" place . . . and remember: those two places are seldom the same.

A Parent Tip

Do the right thing and the safe thing. If you're constantly misbehaving, how can you expect your kids not to.

DURING DARK DAYS

I have heard your prayer, I have seen your tears; behold, I will heal you.

2 KINGS 20:5 NASB

The sadness that accompanies any significant loss is an inevitable fact of life. In time, sadness runs its course and gradually abates. Depression, on the other hand, is a physical and emotional condition that is highly treatable.

If you find yourself feeling "blue," perhaps it's a logical reaction to the ups and downs of daily life. But if you or someone close to you have become dangerously depressed, it's time to seek professional help.

Some days are light and happy, and some days are not. When we face the inevitable dark days of life, we must choose how we will respond. Will we allow ourselves to sink even more deeply into our own sadness, or will we do the difficult work of pulling ourselves out? We bring light to the dark days of life by turning first to God, and then to trusted family members, friends, and medical professionals. When we do, the clouds will eventually part, and the sun will shine once more upon our souls.

A Parent Tip

Depression is serious business, and it's a highly treatable disease . . . treat it that way.

Day 40

TODAY'S OPPORTUNITIES

But encourage one another day after day, as long as it is still called "Today," so that none of you will be hardened by the deceitfulness of sin.

HEBREWS 3:13 NASB

The 118th Psalm reminds us, "This is the day which the Lord hath made; we will rejoice and be glad in it" (v. 24 KJV). As we rejoice in this day that the Lord has given us, let us remember that an important part of today's celebration is the time we spend celebrating others. Each day provides countless opportunities to encourage our loved ones and to praise their good works. When we do, we not only spread seeds of joy and happiness, we also follow the commandments of God's Holy Word.

How can we build others up? By celebrating their victories and their accomplishments. So look for the good in others and celebrate the good that you find. When you do, you'll be a powerful force of encouragement in the world . . . and a worthy servant to your God.

A Quote to Talk About

Encouragement starts at home, but it should never end there.

MARIE T. FREEMAN

HUMBLED BY HIS SACRIFICE

But as for me, I will never boast about anything except the cross of our Lord Jesus Christ, through whom the world has been crucified to me, and I to the world.

GALATIANS 6:14 HCSB

As we consider Christ's sacrifice on the cross, we should be profoundly humbled. And today, as we come to Christ in prayer, we should do so in a spirit of humble devotion.

Christ humbled Himself on a cross—for you and your family. He shed His blood—for you and your family. He has offered to walk with you through this life and throughout all eternity. As you approach Him today in prayer, think about His sacrifice and His grace. And be humble.

A Parent Tip

As an adult, you know that the journey toward spiritual maturity lasts a lifetime. And as a concerned parent, it's up to you to make sure that your child understands that following Christ every day results in a dynamic growing relationship with God.

ETERNAL PERSPECTIVE

Our Savior Jesus poured out new life so generously. God's gift has restored our relationship with him and given us back our lives. And there's more life to come—an eternity of life!

TITUS 3:6-7 MSG

Christ sacrificed His life on the cross so that we might have eternal life. This gift, freely given by God's only begotten Son, is the priceless possession of everyone who accepts Him as Lord and Savior.

As you struggle with the inevitable hardships and occasional disappointments of everyday life, remember that God has invited you to accept His abundance not only for today but also for all eternity. So keep things in perspective. Although you will inevitably encounter occasional defeats in this world, you'll have all eternity to celebrate the ultimate victory in the next.

A Talking Point

Today, talk to your daughter about God's promise of eternal life.

GOD AND FAMILY

Let the Word of Christ—the Message—have the run of the house. Give it plenty of room in your lives.

COLOSSIANS 3:16 MSG

These are difficult days for our nation and for our families. But, thankfully, God is bigger than all of our challenges. God loves us and protects us. In times of trouble, He comforts us; in times of sorrow, He dries our tears. When we are troubled, or weak, or sorrowful, God is as near as our next breath.

Are you concerned for the well-being of your family? You are not alone. We live in a world where temptation and danger seem to lurk on every street corner. Parents and children alike have good reason to be watchful. But, despite the evils of our time, God remains steadfast. Even in these difficult days, no problem is too big for God.

A Parent Tip

Courtesy starts at home. If your children don't learn mannerly behavior at the family dinner table, they won't learn it anywhere else.

Day 44

MAKING TIME FOR GOD

He said to him, "You shall love the Lord your God with all your heart, with all your soul, and with all your mind. This is the greatest and most important commandment."

MATTHEW 22:37-38 HCSB

When it comes to spending time with God, are you a "squeezer" or a "pleaser"? Do you squeeze God into your schedule with a prayer before meals (and maybe, if you've got the time, with a quick visit to church on Sunday)? Or do you please God by talking to Him far more often than that?

If you're wise, and if you want to set a worthy example for your family, you'll form the habit of spending time with God every day. When you do, it will change your focus, your family, and your life.

A Quote to Talk About

Are you weak? Weary? Confused? Troubled? Pressured? How is your relationship with God? Is it held in its place of priority? I believe the greater the pressure, the greater your need for time alone with Him.

KAY ARTHUR

Day 45

BEYOND THE DAILY GRIND

Come unto me, all ye that labor and are heavy laden, and I will give you rest.

MATTHEW 11:28 KJV

Even the most inspired parents can, from time to time, find themselves running on empty. Why? Because the inevitable demands of daily life can drain us of our strength and rob us of the joy that is rightfully ours in Christ. Thankfully, God stands ready to renew our spirits, even on the darkest of days. God's Word is clear: When we genuinely lift our hearts and prayers to Him, He renews our strength.

Are you seeking a renewed sense of purpose? Turn your heart toward God in prayer. Are you weak or worried? Take the time to delve deeply into God's Holy Word. Are you spiritually depleted? Call upon fellow believers to support you, and call upon Christ to renew your spirit and your life. When you do, you'll discover that the Creator of the universe stands always ready and always able to create a new sense of wonderment and joy in you.

A Parent Tip

Be sure you're getting adequate rest. Without it, you'll tend to become easily frustrated, anxious, and irritable. Sleep deprivation makes clear thinking difficult; too much sleep deprivation makes clear thinking impossible.

A FRESH OPPORTUNITY

Therefore we were buried with Him by baptism into death, in order that, just as Christ was raised from the dead by the glory of the Father, so we too may walk in a new way of life.

ROMANS 6:4 HCSB

God's Word is clear: When we genuinely invite Him to reign over our hearts, and when we accept His transforming love, we are forever changed. When we welcome Christ into our hearts, an old life ends and a new way of living—along with a completely new way of viewing the world—begins.

Each morning offers a fresh opportunity to invite Christ, yet once again, to rule over our hearts and our days. Each morning presents yet another opportunity to take up His cross and follow in His footsteps. Today, let us rejoice in the new life that is ours through Christ, and let us follow Him, step by step, on the path that He first walked.

A Talking Point

Today, talk to your daughter about what it means to follow in the footsteps of Jesus.

Day 47

THE CHOICE TO FORGIVE

You have heard that it was said, You shall love your neighbor and hate your enemy. But I tell you, love your enemies, and pray for those who persecute you.

MATTHEW 5:43-44 HCSB

Forgiveness is a choice. We can either choose to forgive those who have injured us, or not. When we obey God by offering forgiveness to His children, we are blessed. But when we allow bitterness and resentment to poison our hearts, we are tortured by our own shortsightedness.

Do you harbor resentment against anyone? If so, you are faced with an important decision: whether or not to forgive the person who has hurt you. God's instructions are clear: He commands you to forgive. And the time to forgive is now because tomorrow may be too late . . . for you.

A Quote to Talk About

Forgiveness is actually the best revenge because it not only sets us free from the person we forgive, but it frees us to move into all that God has in store for us.

STORMIE OMARTIAN

Day 48

THE SEEDS OF GENEROSITY

Freely you have received, freely give.

MATTHEW 10:8 NKJV

Paul reminds us that when we sow the seeds of generosity, we reap bountiful rewards in accordance with God's plan for our lives. Thus, we are instructed to give cheerfully and without reservation: "But this I say, He which soweth sparingly shall reap also sparingly; and he which soweth bountifully shall reap also bountifully. Every man according as he purposeth in his heart, so let him give; not grudgingly, or of necessity: for God loveth a cheerful giver" (2 Corinthians 9:6, 7 KJV).

Today, make this pledge and keep it: Be a cheerful, generous, courageous giver. The world needs your help, and you need the spiritual rewards that will be yours when you give it.

A Quote to Talk About

As faithful stewards of what we have, ought we not to give earnest thought to our staggering surplus?

ELISABETH ELLIOT

TRANSCENDENT LOVE

Who can separate us from the love of Christ? Can affliction or anguish or persecution or famine or nakedness or danger or sword? . . . No, in all these things we are more than victorious through Him who loved us.

ROMANS 8:35, 37 HCSB

Where can we find God's love? Everywhere. God's love transcends space and time. It reaches beyond the heavens, and it touches the darkest, smallest corner of every human heart. When we become passionate in our devotion to the Father, when we sincerely open our minds and hearts to Him, His love does not arrive "some day"—it arrives immediately.

Today, take God at His word and welcome His Son into your heart. When you do, God's transcendent love will surround you and transform you, now and forever.

A Quote to Talk About

There is no pit so deep that God's love is not deeper still.

CORRIE TEN BOOM

Day 50

A PRESCRIPTION FOR PANIC

Anxiety in the heart of man causes depression, but a good word makes it glad.

PROVERBS 12:25 NKJV

We are members of an anxious society, a society in which the changes we face threaten to outpace our abilities to make adjustments. No wonder we sometimes find ourselves beset by feelings of anxiety and panic.

At times, our anxieties may stem from physical causes—chemical imbalances that result in severe emotional distress. In such cases, modern medicine offers hope to those who suffer. But oftentimes, our anxieties result from spiritual deficits, not physical ones. And when we're spiritually depleted, the best prescription is found not in the medicine cabinet but deep inside the human heart. What we need is a higher daily dose of God's love, God's assurance, and God's presence. We acquire these blessings through prayer, through meditation, through worship, and through trust.

A Talking Point

Today, remind your daughter that when she has worries, she should pray about them and she should talk to you about them.

PROMISES YOU CAN COUNT ON

God blesses the people who patiently endure testing. Afterward they will receive the crown of life that God has promised to those who love him.

JAMES 1:12 NLT

Throughout the seasons of life, we must all endure life-altering personal losses that leave us breathless. When we do, we may be overwhelmed by fear, by doubt, or by both. Thankfully, God has promised that He will never desert us. And God keeps His promises.

Life is often challenging, but as Christians, we must trust the promises of our Heavenly Father. God loves us, and He will protect us. In times of hardship, He will comfort us; in times of sorrow, He will dry our tears. When we are troubled, or weak, or sorrowful, God is with us. His love endures, not only for today, but also for all of eternity.

A Parent Tip

Don't be afraid to preach sermons to your daughter, but don't preach her too often. Save your most important lectures for the most important occasions.

Day 52

TAKING TIME TO ASK

God answered their prayers because they trusted him.

1 CHRONICLES 5:20 MSG

Sometimes, amid the demands and the frustrations of everyday life, we forget to slow ourselves down long enough to talk with God. Instead of turning our thoughts and prayers to Him, we rely upon our own resources. Instead of praying for strength and courage, we seek to manufacture it within ourselves. Instead of asking God for guidance, we depend only upon our own limited wisdom. The results of such behaviors are unfortunate and, on occasion, tragic.

Are you in need? Ask God to sustain you. Are you troubled? Take your worries to Him in prayer. Are you weary? Seek God's strength. In all things great and small, seek God's wisdom and His grace. He hears your prayers, and He will answer. All you must do is ask.

A Talking Point

Today, remind your daughter that she should always ask God for the things she needs.

BEYOND OUR REGRETS

Get rid of all bitterness, rage, anger, harsh words, and slander, as well as all types of malicious behavior. Instead, be kind to each other, tenderhearted, forgiving one another, just as God through Christ has forgiven you.

EPHESIANS 4:31-32 NLT

Are you mired in the quicksand of bitterness or regret? If so, you are not only disobeying God's Word, you are also wasting your time. The world holds few if any rewards for those who remain angrily focused upon the past. Still, the act of forgiveness is difficult for all but the most saintly men and women.

Being frail, fallible, imperfect beings, most of us are quick to anger, quick to blame, slow to forgive, and even slower to forget. Yet as Christians, we are commanded to forgive others, just as we, too, have been forgiven.

If there exists even one person—alive or dead—against whom you hold bitter feelings, it's time to forgive. Or, if you are embittered against yourself for some past mistake or shortcoming, it's finally time to forgive yourself and move on. Hatred, bitterness, and regret are not part of God's plan for your life. Forgiveness is.

A Parent Tip

Temper tantrums: If you expect your children to control their tempers then you must also control yours.

Day 54

GOD'S ALLY

Keep a cool head. Stay alert. The Devil is poised to pounce, and would like nothing better than to catch you napping.

1 PETER 5:8 MSG

Nineteenth-century clergyman Edwin Hubbel Chapin warned, "Neutral people are the devil's allies." His words were true then, and they're true now. Neutrality in the face of evil is a sin. Yet all too often, we fail to fight evil, not because we are neutral, but because we are shortsighted: we don't fight the devil because we don't recognize his handiwork.

If we are to recognize evil and fight it, we must pay careful attention. We must pay attention to God's Word, and we must pay attention to the realities of everyday life. When we observe life objectively, and when we do so with eyes and hearts that are attuned to God's Holy Word, we can no longer be neutral believers. And when we are no longer neutral, God rejoices while the devil despairs.

A Quote to Talk About

If we guard some comer of darkness in ourselves, we will soon be drawing someone else into darkness, shutting them out from the light in the face of Jesus Christ.

ELISABETH ELLIOT

IN HIS HANDS

For whatever is born of God overcomes the world. And this is the victory that has overcome the world—our faith.

1 JOHN 5:4 NKJV

The first element of a successful life is faith: faith in God, faith in His Son, and faith in His promises. If we place our lives in God's hands, our faith is rewarded in ways that we—as human beings with clouded vision and limited understanding—can scarcely comprehend. But, if we seek to rely solely upon our own resources, or if we seek earthly success outside the boundaries of God's commandments, we reap a bitter harvest for ourselves and for our loved ones.

Do you desire the abundance and success that God has promised? Then trust Him today and every day that you live. Then, when you have entrusted your future to the Giver of all things good, rest assured that your future is secure, not only for today, but also for all eternity.

A Quote to Talk About

Faith is seeing light with the eyes of your heart, when the eyes of your body see only darkness.

BARBARA JOHNSON

Day 56

THE LAST WORD

For God has not given us a spirit of timidity, but of power and love and discipline. Therefore do not be ashamed of the testimony of our Lord....

2 TIMOTHY 1:7-8 NASB

All of us may find our courage tested by the inevitable disappointments and tragedies of life. After all, ours is a world filled with uncertainty, hardship, sickness, and danger. Old Man Trouble, it seems, is never too far from the front door.

When we focus upon our fears and our doubts, we may find many reasons to lie awake at night and fret about the uncertainties of the coming day. A better strategy, of course, is to focus not upon our fears, but instead upon our God.

God is your shield and your strength; you are His forever. So don't focus your thoughts upon the fears of the day. Instead, trust God's plan and His eternal love for you. And remember: God is good, and He has the last word.

A Quote to Talk About

God shields us from most of the things we fear, but when He chooses not to shield us, He unfailingly allots grace in the measure needed.

ELISABETH ELLIOT

IN THE FOOTSTEPS OF THE SAVIOR

The one who loves his life will lose it, and the one who hates his life in this world will keep it for eternal life. If anyone serves Me, he must follow Me. Where I am, there My servant also will be. If anyone serves Me, the Father will honor him.

JOHN 12:25-26 HCSB

Whom will you walk with today? Will you walk with people who worship the ways of the world? Or will you walk with the Son of God? Jesus walks with you. Are you walking with Him? Hopefully, you will choose to walk with Him today and every day of your life. God's Word promises that when you follow in Christ's footsteps, you will learn how to live freely and lightly (Matthew 11:28-30).

Are you worried about the day ahead? Be confident in God's power. He will never desert you. Are you concerned about the future? Be courageous and call upon God. He will protect you. Are you confused? Listen to the quiet voice of your Heavenly Father. He is not a God of confusion. So talk with God; listen to Him; and walk with His Son—starting now.

A Talking Point

Today, talk to your daughter about the need to honor Jesus, not the world.

Day 58

PERFECT WISDOM

Therefore, everyone who hears these words of Mine and acts on them will be like a sensible man who built his house on the rock. The rain fell, the rivers rose, and the winds blew and pounded that house. Yet it didn't collapse, because its foundation was on the rock.

MATTHEW 7:24-25 HCSB

Where will you and your loved ones place your trust today? Will you trust in the wisdom of fallible men and women, or will you place your faith in God's perfect wisdom? Where you choose to place your trust will determine the direction and quality of your life.

Are you tired? Discouraged? Fearful? Be comforted and trust God. Are you worried or anxious? Be confident in God's power and trust His Holy Word. Are you confused? Listen to the quiet voice of your Father. He is not a God of confusion. Talk with Him; listen to Him; trust Him. He is steadfast, and He is your protector.

A Parent Tip

As parents, we can't make friendships for our children, but we can coach them on the art of making friends. All of us, whether youngsters or grown-ups, make friends by treating others as we wish to be treated. And if that sounds suspiciously like the Golden Rule, that's because it is the Golden Rule.

USING YOUR GIFTS

I remind you to fan into flame the gift of God.

2 TIMOTHY 1:6 NIV

All people possess special gifts—bestowed from the Father above—and you are no exception. But, your gift is no guarantee of success; it must be cultivated and nurtured; otherwise, it will go unused . . . and God's gift to you will be squandered.

Today, make a promise to yourself that you will earnestly seek to discover the talents that God has given you. Then, nourish those talents and make them grow. Finally, vow to share your gifts with the world for as long as God gives you the power to do so. After all, the best way to say "Thank You" for God's gifts is to use them.

A Talking Point

Today, talk to your daughter about the importance of using the gifts God has given her.

Day 60

WHY HE SENT HIS SON

For all have sinned, and fall short of the glory of God, being justified freely by His grace through the redemption that is in Christ Jesus....

ROMANS 3:23-24 NKJV

Despite our shortcomings, God sent His Son so that we might be redeemed from our sins. In doing so, our Heavenly Father demonstrated His infinite mercy and His infinite love. We have received countless gifts from God, but none can compare with the gift of salvation. God's grace is the ultimate gift, and we owe Him the ultimate in thanksgiving.

Christ sacrificed His life on the cross so that we might have eternal life. This gift, freely given from God's only begotten Son, is the priceless possession of everyone who accepts Him as Lord and Savior. We return our Savior's love by welcoming Him into our hearts and sharing His message and His love. When we do so, we are blessed here on earth and throughout all eternity.

A Quote to Talk About

In the depths of our sin, Christ died for us. He did not wait for persons to get as close as possible through obedience to the law and righteous living.

BETH MOORE

OUR ACTIONS AND OUR BELIEFS

As you have therefore received Christ Jesus the Lord, so walk in Him, rooted and built up in Him and established in the faith, as you have been taught, abounding in it with thanksgiving.

COLOSSIANS 2:6-7 NKJV

As Christian parents, we must do our best to make sure that our actions are accurate reflections of our beliefs. We may proclaim our beliefs to our hearts' content, but our proclamations will mean nothing—to others or to ourselves—unless we accompany our words with deeds that match. The sermons that we live are far more compelling than the ones we preach. So remember this: whether you like it or not, your life is an accurate reflection of your creed. If this fact gives you cause for concern, don't bother talking about the changes that you intend to make—make them. And then, when your good deeds speak for themselves—as they most certainly will—don't interrupt.

A Parent Tip

When talking to your children about God, your actions speak much more loudly than your words. So behave accordingly.

Day 62

LIFE'S ROADMAP

All Scripture is inspired by God and is profitable for teaching, for rebuking, for correcting, for training in righteousness, so that the man of God may be complete, equipped for every good work.

2 TIMOTHY 3:16-17 HCSB

Are you sincerely seeking to discover God's will and follow it? If so, study His Word and obey His commandments. The words of Matthew 4:4 remind us that, "Man shall not live by bread alone, but by every word that proceeds from the mouth of God" (NKJV). As believers, we must study the Bible and meditate upon its meaning for our lives. Otherwise, we deprive ourselves of a priceless gift from our Creator.

God's Word is, indeed, a one-of-a-kind treasure, and a passing acquaintance with the Good Book is insufficient for thoughtful parents (like you) who seek to obey God's Word and teach their children to do likewise. And that's good because neither moms, nor dads, nor kids, should be asked to live by bread alone . . .

A Parent Tip

How can you teach your children the importance of God's Holy Word? By example. When teaching your child about the Bible, words are fine—but actually studying your own Bible is far better.

THIS IS HIS DAY

This is the day the LORD has made. We will rejoice and be glad in it.

PSALM 118:24 NLT

The 118th Psalm reminds us that today, like every other day, is a cause for celebration. God gives us this day; He fills it to the brim with possibilities, and He challenges us to use it for His purposes. The day is presented to us fresh and clean at midnight, free of charge, but we must beware: Today is a non-renewable resource—once it's gone, it's gone forever. Our responsibility, of course, is to use this day in the service of God's will and according to His commandments.

If your daughter is like most people, she may, at times, fall victim to the negativity and cynicism of our negative age. And if that happens, it's up to you to remind her that every day is a gift and that she should treasure the time that God has given her.

The Christian life should be a triumphal celebration, a daily exercise in thanksgiving and praise. Encourage your daughter to join that celebration. And while you're at it, make sure that you've joined in the celebration, too.

A Talking Point

Talk to your daughter about the need to celebrate life.

Day 64

CHARACTER-BUILDING TAKES TIME

Because you have these blessings, do your best to add these things to your lives: to your faith, add goodness; and to your goodness, add knowledge; and to your knowledge, add self-control.

2 PETER 1:5-6 NCV

Character is built slowly over a lifetime. It is the sum of every right decision, every honest word, every noble thought, and every heartfelt prayer. It is forged on the anvil of honorable work and polished by the twin virtues of generosity and humility. Character is a precious thing—difficult to build but easy to tear down.

As concerned parents—and as believers in Christ—we must seek to live each day with discipline, honesty, and faith. When we do, integrity becomes a habit. And God smiles.

A Parent Tip

It's hard work being a responsible parent, but the rewards always outweigh the costs. Simply put, your youngster is a marvelous gift from God. And, your opportunity to be a parent is yet another gift, for which you should give thanks.

CHOICES THAT PLEASE GOD

I am offering you life or death, blessings or curses. Now, choose life! . . . To choose life is to love the Lord your God, obey him, and stay close to him.

DEUTERONOMY 30:19-20 NCV

Sometimes, because you're an imperfect human being, you may become so wrapped up in meeting society's expectations that you fail to focus on God's expectations. To do so is a mistake of major proportions—don't make it. Instead, seek God's guidance as you focus your energies on becoming the best "you" that you can possibly be. And, when it comes to matters of conscience, seek approval not from your peers, but from your Creator.

Whom will you try to please today: God or man? Your primary obligation is not to please imperfect men and women. Your obligation is to strive diligently to meet the expectations of an all-knowing and perfect God. Trust Him always. Love Him always. Praise Him always. And make choices that please Him. Always.

A Parent Tip

Big decisions, especially decisions about health and safety, should be made by thoughtful parents, not children.

Day 66

MEASURING YOUR WORDS

A wise heart instructs its mouth and increases learning with its speech.

PROVERBS 16:23 HCSB

God's Word reminds us that "Reckless words pierce like a sword, but the tongue of the wise brings healing" (Proverbs 12:18 NIV). If you seek to be a source of encouragement to friends, to family members, and to coworkers, then you must measure your words carefully.

Today, make this promise to yourself: vow to be an honest, effective, encouraging communicator at home, at work, and everyplace in between. Speak wisely, not impulsively. Use words of kindness and praise, not words of anger or derision. Learn how to be truthful without being cruel. Remember that you have the power to heal others or to injure them, to lift others up or to hold them back. And when you learn how to lift them up, you'll soon discover that you've lifted yourself up, too.

A Parent Tip

Every parent knows that sometimes, a stern lecture is in order. But, every serious conversation between a parent and child should not be an occasion for the gnashing of teeth; parents should engage their children in positive, uplifting, encouraging conversations whenever possible; otherwise, children simply "tune out" their parents.

GOD'S ASSURANCE

I've told you all this so that trusting me, you will be unshakable and assured, deeply at peace. In this godless world you will continue to experience difficulties. But take heart! I've conquered the world.

JOHN 16:33 MSG

Are you a confident believer, or do you live under a cloud of uncertainty and doubt? As a Christian parent, you have many reasons to be confident. After all, God is in His heaven; Christ has risen; and you are the recipient of God's grace. Despite these blessings, you may, from time to time, find yourself being tormented by negative emotions—and you are certainly not alone.

Even the most faithful Christians are overcome by occasional bouts of fear and doubt. You are no different.

But even when you feel very distant from God, remember that God is never distant from you. When you sincerely seek His presence, He will touch your heart, calm your fears, and restore your confidence.

A Talking Point

Today, remind your daughter that the more she trusts God, the more confident she will become.

Day 68

THE STORMS OF LIFE

Immediately Jesus spoke to them. "Have courage! It is I. Don't be afraid."

MATTHEW 14:27 HCSB

A storm rose quickly on the Sea of Galilee, and the disciples were afraid. Although they had seen Jesus perform many miracles, the disciples feared for their lives, so they turned to their Savior, and He calmed the waters and the wind.

Sometimes, we, like the disciples, feel threatened by the inevitable storms of life. And when we are fearful, we, too, can turn to Christ for courage and for comfort.

The next time you're afraid, remember that the One who calmed the wind and the waves is also your personal Savior. And remember that the ultimate battle has already been won at Calvary. We, as believers, can live courageously in the promises of our Lord...and we should.

A Parent Tip

With God as your partner, you have nothing to fear. Why? Because you and God, working together, can handle absolutely anything that comes your way.

LETTING GOD DECIDE

We can make our plans, but the LORD determines our steps.
PROVERBS 16:9 NLT

Are you facing a difficult decision, a troubling circumstance, or a powerful temptation? If so, it's time to step back, to stop focusing on the world, and to focus, instead, on the will of your Father in heaven. The world will often lead you astray, but God will not. His counsel leads you to Himself, which, of course, is the path He has always intended for you to take.

Everyday living is an exercise in decision-making. Today and every day you must make choices: choices about what you will do, what you will worship, and how you will think. When in doubt, make choices that you sincerely believe will bring you to a closer relationship with God. And if you're uncertain of your next step, pray about it. When you do, answers will come—the right answers for you.

A Parent Tip

Christianity is more than a way of worshipping; it's a way of life. For believers—Christian parents and children alike—every day should provide opportunities to honor God by walking in the footsteps of His Son.

Day 70

OUR FAITH, HIS PROMISES

Without wavering, let us hold tightly to the hope we say we have, for God can be trusted to keep his promise.

HEBREWS 10:23 NLT

The Christian faith is founded upon promises that are contained in a unique book. That book is the Holy Bible. The Bible is a roadmap for life here on earth and for life eternal. As Christians, we are called upon to study its meaning, to trust its promises, to follow its commandments, and to share its Good News. God's Holy Word is, indeed, a transforming, one-of-a-kind treasure, and must be treated that way.

Are you facing a difficult decision? Pause for a moment and have a quiet consultation with your ultimate Advisor. Are you fearful, anxious, fretful, or troubled? Slow yourself down long enough to consider the instructions contained in God's Word. These teachings never fail and they never grow old.

Yes, God has made many promises to you and your family . . . and He intends to keep every one of them. So take God at His word: trust His promises and share them with your family, with your friends, and with the world.

A Quote to Talk About

Gather the riches of God's promises which can strengthen you in the time when there will be no freedom.

CORRIE TEN BOOM

TRUSTING HIS TIMING

He told them, "You don't get to know the time. Timing is the Father's business."

ACTS 1:7 MSG

If you sincerely seek to be a person of faith, then you must learn to trust God's timing. You will be sorely tempted, however, to do otherwise. Because you are a fallible human being, you are impatient for things to happen. But, God knows better.

God has created a world that unfolds according to His own timetable, not ours . . . thank goodness! We mortals might make a terrible mess of things.

God's plan does not always happen in the way that we would like or at the time of our own choosing. Our task—as believing Christians who trust in a benevolent, all-knowing Father—is to wait patiently for God to reveal Himself. And reveal Himself He will. Always. But until God's perfect plan is made known, we must walk in faith and never lose hope. And we must continue to trust Him. Always.

A Quote to Talk About

We must leave it to God to answer our prayers in His own wisest way. Sometimes, we are so impatient and think that God does not answer. God always answers! He never fails! Be still. Abide in Him.

MRS. CHARLES E. COWMAN

Day 72

HOW BEST TO TREAT OTHERS

Therefore, whatever you want others to do for you, do also the same for them—this is the Law and the Prophets.

MATTHEW 7:12 HCSB

Would you like to make the world a better place? If so, you can start by practicing the Golden Rule.

Is the Golden Rule your rule, or is it just another Bible verse that goes in one ear and out the other? Jesus made Himself perfectly clear: He instructed you to treat other people in the same way that you want to be treated. But sometimes, especially when you're feeling the pressures or everyday living, obeying the Golden Rule can seem like an impossible task—but it's not. So if you want to know how to treat other people, ask the person you see every time you look into the mirror. The answer you receive will tell you exactly what to do.

A Talking Point

Today, talk to your daughter about the Golden Rule.

HIS JOY . . . AND OURS

Rejoice in the Lord always. I will say it again: Rejoice!

PHILIPPIANS 4:4 HCSB

Christ made it clear: He intends that His joy should become our joy. Yet sometimes, amid the inevitable hustle and bustle of life, we can forfeit—albeit temporarily—the joy of Christ as we wrestle with the challenges of daily living.

Corrie ten Boom correctly observed, "Jesus did not promise to change the circumstances around us. He promised great peace and pure joy to those who would learn to believe that God actually controls all things." So here's a prescription for better spiritual health: Learn to trust God, and open the door of your soul to Christ. When you do, He will most certainly give you the peace and pure joy He has promised.

A Parent Tip

If you want to teach your daughter what it means to be a joyful Christian . . . be one.

Day 74

ALL IN THE FAMILY

Let the message about the Messiah dwell richly among you, teaching and admonishing one another in all wisdom, and singing psalms, hymns, and spiritual songs, with gratitude in your hearts to God.

COLOSSIANS 3:16 HCSB

As every parent knows, family life is a mixture of conversations, mediations, frustrations, commiserations, negotiations and celebrations. In other words, life in a typical family is incredibly varied.

In the life of every family, there are moments of frustration and disappointment. Lots of them. But, for those who are lucky enough to live in the presence of a close-knit, caring clan, the rewards far outweigh the frustrations. That's why we pray fervently for our family members, and that's why we love them despite their faults.

No family is perfect, and neither is yours. But, despite the inevitable challenges and occasional hurt feelings of family life, your clan is God's gift to you. That little band of men, women, kids, and babies is a priceless treasure on temporary loan from the Father above. Give thanks to God for your family . . . and act accordingly.

A Quote to Talk About

Never give your family the leftovers and crumbs of your time.

CHARLES SWINDOLL

THE FINANCIAL GUIDE

The blessing of the Lord makes one rich . . . .

PROVERBS 10:22 NKJV

God's Word is not only a roadmap to eternal life, it is also an indispensable guidebook for life here on earth. As such, the Bible has much to say about your life and your finances.

God's Word can be a roadmap to a place of righteousness and abundance. Make it your roadmap. God's wisdom can be a light to guide your steps. Claim it as your light. God's Word can be an invaluable tool for crafting a better day and a better life. Make it your tool. And finally, God's Word can help you organize your financial life in such a way that you have less need to worry and more time to celebrate His glorious creation. If that sounds appealing, open your Bible, read its instructions, and follow them.

A Parent Tip

Your future depends, to a very great extent, upon how much you are willing to invest in yourself. So keep learning and keep growing personally, professionally, and spiritually.

Day 76

LOVE THAT FORGIVES

And whenever you stand praying, if you have anything against anyone, forgive him, so that your Father in heaven may also forgive you your wrongdoing.

MARK 11:25 HCSB

Genuine love is an exercise in forgiveness. If we wish to build lasting relationships, we must learn how to forgive. Why? Because our loved ones are imperfect (as are we). How often must we forgive our family and friends? More times than we can count. Why? Because that's what God wants us to do.

Perhaps granting forgiveness is hard for you. If so, you are not alone. Genuine, lasting forgiveness is often difficult to achieve—difficult but not impossible. Thankfully, with God's help, all things are possible, and that includes forgiveness. But, even though God is willing to help, He expects you to do some of the work. And make no mistake: forgiveness is work, which is okay with God. He knows that the payoffs are worth the effort.

A Parent Tip

You are an example; be a good one. Your children will learn how to treat others by watching you; be kindhearted, understanding, and forgiving to everyone, starting with the precious people who live under your roof.

IN HIS HANDS

Don't brashly announce what you're going to do tomorrow; you don't know the first thing about tomorrow.

PROVERBS 27:1 MSG

The old saying is both familiar and true: "Man proposes and God disposes." Our world unfolds according to God's plans, not our wishes. Thus, boasting about future events is to be avoided by those who acknowledge God's sovereignty over all things.

Are you planning for a better tomorrow for yourself and your family? If so, you are to be congratulated: God rewards forethought in the same way that He often punishes impulsiveness. But as you make your plans, do so with humility, with gratitude, and with trust in your Heavenly Father. His hand directs the future; to think otherwise is both arrogant and naïve.

A Parent Tip

Worried about your family or your future? Since God has promised to guide and protect you—now and forever—you should never lose hope.

Day 78

GOD IS LOVE

We know how much God loves us, and we have put our trust in him. God is love, and all who live in love live in God, and God lives in them.

1 JOHN 4:16 NLT

The Bible makes this promise: God is love. It's a sweeping statement, a profoundly important description of what God is and how God works. God's love is perfect. When we open our hearts to His perfect love, we are touched by the Creator's hand, and we are transformed.

Today, even if you can only carve out a few quiet moments, offer sincere prayers of thanksgiving to your Creator. He loves you now and throughout all eternity. Open your heart to His presence and His love.

A Quote to Talk About

Let's never forget that some of God's greatest mercies are His refusals. He says no in order that He may, in some way we cannot imagine, say yes. All His ways with us are merciful. His meaning is always love.

ELISABETH ELLIOT

TRUST HIM TO GUIDE YOU

Trust in the Lord with all your heart, and do not rely on your own understanding; think about Him in all your ways, and He will guide you on the right paths.

PROVERBS 3:5-6 HCSB

As Christians whose salvation has been purchased by the blood of Christ, we have every reason to live joyously and courageously. After all, Christ has already fought and won our battle for us—He did so on the cross at Calvary. But despite Christ's sacrifice, and despite God's promises, we may become confused or disoriented by the endless complications and countless distractions of modern life.

If you're unsure of your next step, lean upon God's promises and lift your prayers to Him. Remember that God is your protector. Open yourself to His heart, and trust Him to guide you. When you do, God will direct your steps, and you will receive His blessings today, tomorrow, and throughout eternity.

A Parent Tip

Have a few important rules and enforce them: No matter how old your children are, they still need to abide by your rules if they want to reside under your roof.

Day 80

ULTIMATE PROTECTION

What time I am afraid, I will trust in thee.

PSALM 56:3 KJV

God has promised to protect us, and He intends to fulfill His promise. In a world filled with dangers and temptations, God is the ultimate armor. In a world filled with misleading messages, God's Word is the ultimate truth. In a world filled with more frustrations than we can count, God's Son offers the ultimate peace.

Will you accept God's peace and wear God's armor against the dangers of our world? Hopefully so, because when you do, you can live courageously, knowing that you possess the ultimate protection: God's unfailing love for you.

A Quote to Talk About

Our future may look fearfully intimidating, yet we can look up to the Engineer of the Universe, confident that nothing escapes His attention or slips out of the control of those strong hands.

ELISABETH ELLIOT

SEEKING GOD AND FINDING HAPPINESS

Happy is the one whose help is the God of Jacob, whose hope is in the Lord his God.

PSALM 146:5 HCSB

Happiness depends less upon our circumstances than upon our thoughts. When we turn our thoughts to God, to His gifts, and to His glorious creation, we experience the joy that God intends for His children. But, when we focus on the negative aspects of life, we suffer needlessly.

Do you sincerely want to be a happy parent and a joyful Christian? Then set your mind and your heart upon God's love and His grace. The fullness of life in Christ is available to all who seek it and claim it. Count yourself among that number. Seek first the salvation that is available through a personal relationship with Jesus Christ, and then claim the joy, the peace, and the spiritual abundance that the Shepherd offers His sheep.

A Parent Tip

Do you want to make your home life a continual feast? Learn to laugh and love, but not necessarily in that order.

Day 82

TRUST THE SHEPHERD

The Lord is my shepherd; I shall not want. He makes me to lie down in green pastures; He leads me beside the still waters. He restores my soul.

PSALM 23:1-3 NKJV

In the 23rd Psalm, David teaches us that God is like a watchful shepherd caring for His flock. No wonder these verses have provided comfort and hope for generations of believers.

As a busy parent, you know from firsthand experience that life is not always easy. But as a recipient of God's grace, you also know that you are protected by a loving Heavenly Father. On occasion, you will confront circumstances that trouble you to the very core of your soul. When you are afraid, trust in God. When you are worried, turn your concerns over to Him. When you are anxious, be still and listen for the quiet assurance of God's promises. And then, place your life in His hands.

A Quote to Talk About

The Lord God of heaven and earth, the Almighty Creator of all things, He who holds the universe in His hand as though it were a very little thing, He is your Shepherd, and He has charged Himself with the care and keeping of you, as a shepherd is charged with the care and keeping of his sheep.

HANNAH WHITALL SMITH

OUR ROCK

My God is my rock, in whom I take refuge, my shield and the horn of my salvation.

2 SAMUEL 22:2-3 NIV

Psalm 145 promises, "The Lord is near to all who call on him, to all who call on him in truth. He fulfills the desires of those who fear him; he hears their cry and saves them" (vv. 18-20 NIV). And the words of Jesus offer us comfort: "These things I have spoken to you, that in Me you may have peace. In the world you will have tribulation; but be of good cheer, I have overcome the world" (John 16:33 NKJV).

As believers, we know that God loves us and that He will protect us. In times of hardship, He will comfort us; in times of sorrow, He will dry our tears. When we are troubled, or weak, or sorrowful, God is always with us. We must build our lives on the rock that cannot be shaken: we must trust in God. And then, we must get on with the hard work of tackling our problems . . . because if we don't, who will? Or should?

A Parent Tip

Don't be afraid to talk with your daughter about your core beliefs, and never be afraid to discuss matters of personal safety or health. But, don't make your sermons too frequent or too condescending.

Day 84

WHEN MOUNTAINS MOVE

You do not have, because you do not ask God.

JAMES 4:2 NIV

God gives the gifts; we, as believers, should accept them—but oftentimes, we don't. Why? Because we fail to trust our Heavenly Father completely, and because we are, at times, surprisingly stubborn. Luke 11 teaches us that God does not withhold spiritual gifts from those who ask. Our obligation, quite simply, is to ask for them.

Are you a parent who asks God to move mountains in your life, or are you expecting Him to stumble over molehills? Whatever the size of your challenges, God is big enough to handle them. Ask for His help today, with faith and with fervor, and then watch in amazement as your mountains begin to move.

A Talking Point

Today, remind your daughter that the best way to thank God for His gifts is to use them.

BELIEVING MAKES A DIFFERENCE

You never saw him, yet you love him. You still don't see him, yet you trust him—with laughter and singing. Because you kept on believing, you'll get what you're looking forward to: total salvation.

1 PETER 1:8-9 MSG

If you'd like to partake in the peace that only God can give, make certain that your actions are guided by His Word. And while you're at it, pay careful attention to the conscience that God, in His infinite wisdom, has placed in your heart. Don't treat your faith as if it were separate from your everyday life. Weave your beliefs into the very fabric of your day. When you do, God will honor your good works, and your good works will honor God.

If you seek to be a responsible believer, you must realize that it is never enough to hear the instructions of God; you must also live by them. And it is never enough to wait idly by while others do God's work; you, too, must act. Doing God's work is a responsibility that every Christian should bear. And when you do, your loving Father will reward your efforts with a bountiful harvest.

A Talking Point

Today, talk to your daughter about the importance of making her actions conform to her beliefs.

Day 86

HEARING THE CALL

One thing I do, forgetting those things which are behind and reaching forward to those things which are ahead, I press toward the goal for the prize of the upward call of God in Christ Jesus.

PHILIPPIANS 3:13-14 NKJV

It is vitally important that you heed God's call. In John 15:16, Jesus says, "You did not choose me, but I chose you and appointed you to go and bear fruit—fruit that will last" (NIV). In other words, you have been called by Christ, and now, it is up to you to decide precisely how you will answer.

Have you already found your special calling? If so, you're a very lucky person. If not, keep searching and keep praying until you discover it. And remember this: God has important work for you to do—work that no one else on earth can accomplish but you.

A Parent Tip

Remember that your daughter has lots of friends but only a couple of parents. So whatever you do, don't abandon your paternal responsibilities . . . your daughter needs a parent more than a pal.

A PATTERN OF GOOD WORKS

In all things showing yourself to be a pattern of good works; in doctrine showing integrity, reverence, incorruptibility . . . .

TITUS 2:7 NKJV

It has been said that character is what we are when nobody is watching. How true. When we do things that we know aren't right, we try to hide them from our families and friends. But even then, God is watching.

If you sincerely wish to walk with God—and if you'd like your children to follow your example—you must seek, to the best of your ability, to follow God's commandments. When you do, your character will take care of itself...and you won't need to look over your shoulder to see who, besides God, is watching.

A Talking Point

Today, remind your daughter that it's important to associate with people who are upbeat, optimistic, and encouraging.

Day 88

A RELATIONSHIP THAT HONORS GOD

I am always praising you; all day long I honor you.

PSALM 71:8 NCV

As you think about the nature of your relationship with God, remember this: you will always have some type of relationship with Him—it is inevitable that your life must be lived in relationship to God. The question is not if you will have a relationship with Him; the burning question is whether or not that relationship will be one that seeks to honor Him.

Are you willing to place God first in your life? And, are you willing to welcome God's Son into your heart? Unless you can honestly answer these questions with a resounding yes, then your relationship with God isn't what it could be or should be. Thankfully, God is always available, He's always ready to forgive, and He's waiting to hear from you now. The rest, of course, is up to you.

A Talking Point

Today, talk to your daughter about her relationship with Jesus.

A PLACE OF WORSHIP

For where two or three are gathered together in My name, I am there among them.

MATTHEW 18:20 HCSB

In the Book of Acts, Luke reminds us to "feed the church of God" (20:28). As Christians who have been saved by a loving, compassionate Creator, we are compelled not only to worship Him in our hearts but also to worship Him in the presence of fellow believers.

We live in a world that is teeming with temptations and distractions—a world where good and evil struggle in a constant battle to win our hearts and souls. Our challenge, of course, is to ensure that we cast our lot on the side of God. One way to ensure that we do so is by the practice of regular, purposeful worship with our families. When we worship God faithfully and fervently, we are blessed.

A Parent Tip

Christ made incredible sacrifices for mankind. What sacrifices will you and your family make today for Him?

Day 90

BLESSINGS FROM ABOVE

I said to myself, "Relax and rest. God has showered you with blessings."

PSALM 116:7 MSG

Psalm 145 makes this promise: "The LORD is gracious and compassionate, slow to anger and rich in love. The LORD is good to all; he has compassion on all he has made" (vv. 8-9 NIV). As God's children, we are blessed beyond measure, but sometimes, as busy parents living in a demanding world, we are slow to count our gifts and even slower to give thanks to the Giver. Our blessings include life and health, family and friends, freedom and possessions—for starters. And, the gifts we receive from God are multiplied when we share them with others. May we always give thanks to God for our blessings, and may we always demonstrate our gratitude by sharing them.

A Parent Tip

God has given you more blessings than you can count. Your job is to accept them and be grateful.

OUR PRICELESS TREASURES

The promise is for you and your children.

ACTS 2:39 NASB

As Christian parents, we are aware that God has entrusted us with priceless treasures from above—our children. Every child is a glorious gift from the Father. And, with the Father's gift comes profound responsibilities. Thoughtful moms and dads understand the critical importance of raising their children with love, with family, with discipline, and with God.

Today, thank the Creator for your family, and do whatever you can to nourish that gift. This is the day the Lord has made: a day to love and treasure your family.

A Parent Tip

Popular culture encourages mixed messages. As a Christian parent, your message must not be mixed; you must focus on Jesus.

Day 92

OUR ULTIMATE SAVIOR

And we have seen and testify that the Father has sent his Son to be the Savior of the world.

1 JOHN 4:14 NIV

Hannah Whitall Smith spoke to believers of every generation when she advised, "Keep your face upturned to Christ as the flowers do to the sun. Look, and your soul shall live and grow." How true. When we turn our hearts to Jesus, we receive His blessings, His peace, and His grace.

Christ is the ultimate Savior of mankind and the personal Savior of those who believe in Him. As His servants, we should place Him at the very center of our lives. And, every day that God gives us breath, we should share Christ's love and His message with a world that needs both.

A Parent Tip

Every family is built upon something; let the foundation of your family be the love of God and the salvation of Christ.

CONTAGIOUS FAITH

Whatever you do, do your work heartily, as for the Lord rather than for men.

COLOSSIANS 3:23 NASB

Genuine, heartfelt Christianity is contagious. If you enjoy a life-altering relationship with God, that relationship will have an impact on others—perhaps a profound impact.

Are you genuinely excited about your faith? And do you make your enthusiasm known to those around you? Or are you a "silent ambassador" for Christ? God's preference is clear: He intends that you stand before others and proclaim your faith.

Does Christ reign over your life? Then share your testimony and your excitement. The world needs both.

A Parent Tip

It all starts with parents: Kindness, dignity, and respect for others begins at the head of the household and works its way down from there.

Day 94

GOD'S VOICE

For God is pleased with you when, for the sake of your conscience, you patiently endure unfair treatment.

1 PETER 2:19 NLT

Billy Graham correctly observed, "Most of us follow our conscience as we follow a wheelbarrow. We push it in front of us in the direction we want to go." To do so, of course, is a profound mistake. Yet all of us, on occasion, have failed to listen to the voice that God planted in our hearts, and all of us have suffered the consequences.

God gave you a conscience for a very good reason: to make your path conform to His will. Wise believers make it a practice to listen carefully to that quiet internal voice. Count yourself among that number. When your conscience speaks, listen and learn. In all likelihood, God is trying to get His message through. And in all likelihood, it is a message that you desperately need to hear.

A Parent Tip

You don't have to haul your daughter to a deserted island to have a meaningful conversation. Meaningful moments between you and your child can happen anywhere—and it's up to you to make sure that they do.

Day 95

GOD CAN HANDLE IT

Fear not, for I have redeemed you; I have called you by your name; You are Mine.

ISAIAH 43:1 NKJV

Life can be difficult and discouraging at times. During our darkest moments, God offers us strength and courage if we turn our hearts and our prayers to Him.

As believing Christians, we have every reason to live courageously. After all, the ultimate battle has already been fought and won on the cross at Calvary. But sometimes, because we are imperfect human beings who possess imperfect faith, we fall prey to fear and doubt. The answer to our fears, of course, is God.

The next time you find your courage tested to the limit, remember that God is as near as your next breath. He is your shield and your strength; He is your protector and your deliverer. Call upon Him in your hour of need and then be comforted. Whatever your challenge, whatever your trouble, God can handle it . . . and will!

A Parent Tip

The road of life contains a number of potholes and stumbling blocks. You will encounter them from time to time, and so will your family members. But, don't invest large quantities of your life focusing on past misfortunes. On the road of life, regret is a dead end.

Day 96

LIMITLESS POWER, LIMITLESS LOVE

I pray also that you will have greater understanding in your heart so you will know the hope to which he has called us and that you will know how rich and glorious are the blessings God has promised his holy people. And you will know that God's power is very great for us who believe.

EPHESIANS 1:18-19 NCV

Because God's power is limitless, it is far beyond the comprehension of mortal minds. Yet even though we cannot fully understand the awesome power of God, we can praise it. When we worship God with faith and assurance, when we place Him at the absolute center of our lives, we invite His love into our hearts. In turn, we grow to love Him more deeply as we sense His love for us.

Let us pray that we, too, will turn our hearts to the Creator, knowing with certainty that His heart has ample room for each of us, and that we, in turn, must make room in our hearts for Him.

A Parent Tip

God is still working in you and through you. Even if you're a mature Christian, you can still grow in the knowledge and love of your Savior every day that you live. And, if you seek to be a righteous example to your children, that's exactly what you will do.

THY WILL BE DONE

"Father, if it is Your will, take this cup away from Me; nevertheless not My will, but Yours, be done."

LUKE 22:42 NKJV

Before His crucifixion, Jesus went to the Mount of Olives and poured out His heart to God. Jesus knew of the agony that He was destined to endure, but He also knew that God's will must be done. We, like our Savior, face trials that bring fear and trembling to the very depths of our souls, but like Christ, we, too, must ultimately seek God's will, not our own. When we entrust our lives to Him completely and without reservation, He gives us the strength to meet any challenge, the courage to face any trial, and the wisdom to live in His righteousness.

A Quote to Talk About

The center of power is not to be found in summit meetings or in peace conferences. It is not in Peking or Washington or the United Nations, but rather where a child of God prays in the power of the Spirit for God's will to be done in her life, in her home, and in the world around her.

RUTH BELL GRAHAM

Day 98

DILIGENCE NOW

Do not lack diligence; be fervent in spirit; serve the Lord.

ROMANS 12:11 HCSB

God's Word reminds us again and again that our Creator expects us to lead disciplined lives. God doesn't reward laziness, misbehavior, or apathy. To the contrary, He expects believers to behave with dignity and discipline.

We live in a world in which leisure is glorified and indifference is often glamorized. But God has other plans. He did not create us for lives of mediocrity; He created us for far greater things. Life's greatest rewards seldom fall into our laps; to the contrary, our greatest accomplishments usually require lots of work, which is perfectly fine with God. After all, He knows that we're up to the task, and He has big plans for us; may we, as disciplined believers, always be worthy of those plans.

A Parent Tip

As a responsible parent, it's up to you to be your family's safety expert. Impulsive kids, left to their own devices, tend to get themselves into dangerous situations; responsible adults, however, don't leave kids to their own devices.

HOPE FOR TODAY, HOPE FOR TOMORROW

This hope we have as an anchor of the soul, a hope both sure and steadfast.

HEBREWS 6:19 NASB

Despite God's promises, despite Christ's love, and despite our countless blessings, we frail human beings can still lose hope from time to time. When we do, we need the encouragement of Christian friends, the life-changing power of prayer, and the healing truth of God's Holy Word. If we find ourselves falling into the spiritual traps of worry and discouragement, we should seek the healing touch of Jesus and the encouraging words of fellow Christians. Even though this world can be a place of trials and struggles, God has promised us peace, joy, and eternal life if we give ourselves to Him. And, of course, God keeps His promises today, tomorrow, and forever.

A Quote to Talk About

Hope looks for the good in people, opens doors for people, discovers what can be done to help, lights a candle, does not yield to cynicism. Hope sets people free.

BARBARA JOHNSON

Day 100

KNOWLEDGE AND WISDOM

A house is built by wisdom, and it is established by understanding; by knowledge the rooms are filled with every precious and beautiful treasure.

PROVERBS 24:3-4 HCSB

If we are to grow as Christians and as parents, we need both knowledge and wisdom. Knowledge is found in the classroom. Wisdom, on the other hand, is found in God's Holy Word and in the carefully chosen words of family members and friends. Knowledge is an important building block in a well-lived life, and it pays rich dividends both personally and professionally. But, wisdom is even more important because it refashions not only the mind, but also the heart.

A Quote to Talk About

A big difference exists between a head full of knowledge and the words of God literally abiding in us.

BETH MOORE

NO COMPLAINTS

Do everything without grumbling and arguing, so that you may be blameless and pure.

PHILIPPIANS 2:14-15 HCSB

Because we are imperfect human beings, we often lose sight of our blessings. Ironically, most of us have more blessings than we can count, but we may still find reasons to complain about the minor frustrations of everyday life. To do so, of course, is not only wrong; it is also the pinnacle of shortsightedness and a serious roadblock on the path to spiritual abundance.

Are you tempted to complain about the inevitable minor frustrations of everyday living? Don't do it! Today and every day, make it a practice to count your blessings, not your hardships. It's the truly decent way to live.

A Parent Tip

Constant complaining is a bad habit—make sure it's not your bad habit!

Day 102

THE WISDOM TO OBEY

And this world is fading away, along with everything it craves. But if you do the will of God, you will live forever.

1 JOHN 2:17 NLT

Since God created Adam and Eve, we human beings have been rebelling against our Creator. Why? Because we are unwilling to trust God's Word, and we are unwilling to follow His commandments. God has given us a guidebook for righteous living called the Holy Bible. It contains thorough instructions which, if followed, lead to fulfillment, righteousness and salvation. But, if we choose to ignore God's commandments, the results are as predictable as they are tragic.

Talking about God is easy; living by His commandments is considerably harder. But, unless we are willing to abide by God's laws, all of our righteous proclamations ring hollow. How can we best proclaim our love for the Lord? By obeying Him. And, for further instructions, read the manual.

A Parent Tip

If your children don't learn obedience between the four walls of your home, they probably won't learn it anywhere else.

UNDER PRESSURE

Obviously, I'm not trying to be a people pleaser! No, I am trying to please God. If I were still trying to please people, I would not be Christ's servant.

GALATIANS 1:10 NLT

Our world is filled with pressures: some good, some bad. The pressures that we feel to follow God's will and obey His commandments are positive pressures. God places them on our hearts, and He intends that we act in accordance with His leadings. But we also face different pressures, ones that are definitely not from God. When we feel pressured to do things—or even to think thoughts—that lead us away from God, we must beware.

Society seeks to mold us into more worldly beings; God seeks to mold us into new beings that are most certainly not conformed to this world. If we are to please God, we must resist the pressures that society seeks to impose upon us, and we must conform ourselves, instead, to God's will, to His path, and to His Son.

A Parent Tip

Teenage years are especially fraught with peer pressure. Young adults can be very sensitive, and they feel rejected at times. As a parent, you find it tempting to lecture your teen endlessly. Resist that temptation. Simply be there, and do more listening than talking.

Day 104

SHARING THE GOOD NEWS

Christ did not send me to baptize people but to preach the Good News. And he sent me to preach the Good News without using words of human wisdom so that the cross of Christ would not lose its power.

1 CORINTHIANS 1:17 NCV

In his second letter to Timothy, Paul offers a message to believers of every generation when he writes, "God has not given us a spirit of timidity" (1:7 NASB). Paul's meaning is crystal clear: When sharing our testimonies, we, as Christians, must be courageous, forthright, and unashamed.

We live in a world that desperately needs the healing message of Christ Jesus. Every believer, each in his or her own way, bears a personal responsibility for sharing that message.

You know how Christ has touched your heart and changed your life. Now it's your turn to share the Good News with others. And remember: today is the perfect time to share your testimony because tomorrow may quite simply be too late.

A Quote to Talk About

Claim the joy that is yours. Pray. And know that your joy is used by God to reach others.

KAY ARTHUR

SEEKING AND FINDING

Keep asking, and it will be given to you. Keep searching, and you will find. Keep knocking, and the door will be opened to you. For everyone who asks receives, and the one who searches finds, and to the one who knocks, the door will be opened.

MATTHEW 7:7-8 HCSB

Where is God? He is everywhere you have ever been and everywhere you will ever go. He is with you night and day; He knows your every thought; He hears your every heartbeat.

Sometimes, in the crush of your daily duties, God may seem far away. Or sometimes, when the disappointments and sorrows of life leave you brokenhearted, God may seem distant, but He is not. When you earnestly seek God, you will find Him because He is here, waiting patiently for you to reach out to Him . . . right here . . . right now.

A Parent Tip

Being a wise parent requires more than knowledge. Knowledge comes from text books, but wisdom comes from God. Wisdom begins with a thorough understanding of God's moral order, the eternal truths that are found in God's Holy Word.

Day 106

BEYOND NEGATIVITY

God is striding ahead of you. He's right there with you. He won't let you down; he won't leave you. Don't be intimidated. Don't worry.

DEUTERONOMY 31:8 MSG

God offers us the strength to meet our challenges, and He offers us hope for the future. One way that He shares His message of hope is through the words of encouraging friends and family members.

Hope, like other human emotions, is contagious. If we associate with hope-filled, enthusiastic people, their enthusiasm will have a tendency to lift our spirits. But if we find ourselves spending too much time in the company of naysayers, pessimists, or cynics, our thoughts—like the naysayers'—will tend to be negative.

Are you a hopeful, optimistic Christian? And do you associate with like-minded people? If so, then you're both wise and blessed.

A Quote to Talk About

The most profane word we use is "hopeless." When you say a situation or person is hopeless, you are slamming the door in the face of God.

KATHY TROCCOLI

GETTING IT ALL DONE

Everyone was trying to touch him—so much energy surging from him, so many people healed!

LUKE 6:19 MSG

All of us have moments when we feel drained. All of us suffer through difficult days, trying times, and perplexing periods of our lives. During times of hardship, we are tempted to burn the candle at both ends, but we should resist this temptation. Instead, we should strive to place first things first by saying no to the things that we simply don't have the time or the energy to do.

If you're a parent with too many demands and too few hours in which to meet them, don't fret. Instead, focus upon God and upon His love for you. Then, ask Him for the wisdom to prioritize your life and the strength to fulfill your responsibilities. God will give you the energy to do the most important things on today's to-do list.

A Quote to Talk About

When the dream of our heart is one that God has planted there, a strange happiness flows into us. At that moment, all of the spiritual resources of the universe are released to help us. Our praying is then at one with the will of God and becomes a channel for the Creator's purposes for us and our world.

CATHERINE MARSHALL

Day 108

YOUR POWERFUL EXAMPLE

We're Christ's representatives. God uses us to persuade men and women to drop their differences and enter into God's work of making things right between them. We're speaking for Christ himself now: Become friends with God; he's already a friend with you.

2 CORINTHIANS 5:20 MSG

Whether you realize it or not, you are a powerful example for your children to follow. And whether you realize it or not, your family is learning far more from the life you live than from the words you say. This raises an important question: what sort of example are you? Are you the kind of believer whose words and deeds are consistent? And do those words and deeds honor the One who gave His life on a cross so that you might enjoy life eternal? Hopefully so!

As you encounter the challenges of everyday living, you will have many opportunities to serve as an enduring example of righteousness. Seize those opportunities now, because your family is carefully watching—and constantly learning.

A Parent Tip

Live according to the principles you teach. The sermons you live are far more important than the sermons you preach.

THE INNER VOICE

Let us come near to God with a sincere heart and a sure faith, because we have been made free from a guilty conscience, and our bodies have been washed with pure water.

HEBREWS 10:22 NCV

American humorist Josh Billings observed, "Reason often makes mistakes, but conscience never does." How true. Even when we deceive our neighbors, and even when we attempt to deceive ourselves, God has given each of us a conscience, a small, quiet voice that tells us right from wrong.

We must listen to that inner voice . . . or else we must accept the consequences that inevitably befall those who choose to rebel against God.

A Talking Point

Today, talk to your daughter about the rewards of listening carefully to her conscience.

Day 110

HOPE FOR THE JOURNEY

So we can be sure when we say, "I will not be afraid, because the Lord is my helper. People can't do anything to me."

HEBREWS 13:6 NCV

Because we are saved by a risen Christ, we can have hope for the future, no matter how desperate our circumstances may seem. After all, God has promised that we are His throughout eternity. And, He has told us that we must place our hopes in Him.

Today, summon the courage to follow God. Even if the path seems difficult, even if your heart is fearful, trust your Heavenly Father and follow Him. Trust Him with your day and your life. Do His work, care for His children, and share His Good News. Let Him guide your steps. He will not lead you astray.

A Talking Point

Today, talk to your daughter about the rewards of living courageously.

DEALING WITH DISAPPOINTMENT

I think you ought to know, dear brothers and sisters, about the trouble we went through in the province of Asia. We were crushed and completely overwhelmed, and we thought we would never live through it. In fact, we expected to die. But as a result, we learned not to rely on ourselves, but on God who can raise the dead. And he did deliver us from mortal danger. And we are confident that he will continue to deliver us.

2 CORINTHIANS 1:8–10 NLT

From time to time, all of us face life-altering disappointments that leave us breathless. Oftentimes, these disappointments come unexpectedly, leaving us with more questions than answers. But even when we don't have all the answers—or, for that matter, even when we don't seem to have any of the answers—God does. Whatever our circumstances, whether we stand atop the highest mountain or wander through the darkest valley, God is ready to protect us, to comfort us, and to heal us. Our task is to let Him.

A Parent Tip

Self-esteem is contagious. So, if you want your daughter to admire the person she sees in the mirror, then you should admire the person you see in the mirror.

Day 112

HIS HEALING TOUCH

I am the Lord who heals you.

EXODUS 15:26 NCV

Are you concerned about your family's spiritual, physical, or emotional health? If so, there is a timeless source of comfort and assurance that is as near your bookshelf. That source is the Holy Bible.

God's Word has much to say about every aspect of your life, including your health. And, when you face concerns of any sort—including health-related challenges—God is with you. So trust your medical doctor to do his or her part, but place your ultimate trust in your benevolent Heavenly Father. His healing touch, like His love, endures forever.

A Parent Tip

Even when certain conversations make you a little bit uncomfortable, keep talking. Your daughter needs your input, and even more importantly, she needs to know that you care enough to give your input.

SELF-MADE?

Respecting the Lord and not being proud will bring you wealth, honor, and life.

PROVERBS 22:4 NCV

We have heard it said on countless occasions: "He's a self-made man," or "She's a self-made woman." In truth, none of us are self-made. We all owe countless debts that we can never repay. Our first debt, of course, is to our Father in heaven—Who has given us everything that we are and will ever be—and to His Son Who sacrificed His own life so that we might live eternally. We are also indebted to ancestors, parents, teachers, friends, spouses, family members, co-workers, fellow believers . . . and the list goes on.

Most of us, it seems, are more than willing to stick out our chests and say, "Look at me; I did that!" But in our better moments, in the quiet moments when we search the depths of our own hearts, we know better. Whatever "it" is, God did that. He deserves the credit.

A Quote to Talk About

That some of my hymns have been dictated by the blessed Holy Spirit I have no doubt; and that others have been the result of deep meditation I know to be true; but that the poet has any right to claim special merit for himself is certainly presumptuous.

FANNY CROSBY

Day 114

LISTEN CAREFULLY

Wise people can also listen and learn.

PROVERBS 1:5 NCV

For many parents, the temptation to lecture their children is almost irresistible. But oftentimes, it's more helpful to listen than to lecture.

God's Word instructs us to be quick to listen and slow to speak. And when it comes to the important job of raising the next generation and strengthening our families, we're wise to listen carefully (first) and then offer helpful words (next).

Perhaps God gave us two ears and one mouth for a reason: so that we might listen twice as much as we speak. After all, listening quietly to our kids can be a wonderful form of encouragement. Besides, after we've listened carefully to our youngsters, we're more likely to respond wisely, not impulsively.

So remember that, as a parent, you have the power to guide your child with your words and your ears. And remember that the words you don't speak can be just as helpful as the ones you do speak.

A Parent Tip

For most parents, the temptation to lecture is great; it takes conscious effort to hold one's tongue until one's ears are fully engaged. When a parent is able to do so, his or her efforts are usually rewarded.

BEYOND MATERIALISM

For what does it benefit a man to gain the whole world yet lose his life? What can a man give in exchange for his life?

MARK 8:36-37 HCSB

In our modern society, we need money to live. But as Christians, we must never make the acquisition of money the central focus of our lives. Money is a tool, but it should never overwhelm our sensibilities. The focus of life must be squarely on things spiritual, not things material.

Whenever we place our love for material possessions above our love for God—or when we yield to the countless other temptations of everyday living—we find ourselves engaged in a struggle between good and evil. Let us respond to this struggle by freeing ourselves from that subtle yet powerful temptation: the temptation to love the world more than we love God.

A Parent Tip

Your family's collective self-esteem starts at the head of the household and works its way down from there. It's not enough to concern yourself with your child's self-image; you should also strive to become comfortable with your own self-image, too.

Day 116

BLESSED OBEDIENCE

When you and your children return to the LORD your God and obey him with all your heart and with all your soul according to everything I command you today, then the LORD your God will restore your fortunes and have compassion on you and gather you again from all the nations where he scattered you.

DEUTERONOMY 30:2-3 NIV

We live in a world filled with temptations, distractions, and countless opportunities to disobey God. But as parents who seek to be godly role models for our children, we must turn our thoughts and our hearts away from the evils of this world. We must turn instead to God.

Talking about God is easy; living by His laws is considerably harder. But unless we are willing to live obediently, all our righteous words ring hollow.

How can we best proclaim our love for the Lord? By obeying Him. We must seek God's counsel and trust the counsel He gives. And, when we invite God into our hearts and live according to His commandments, we are blessed today, and tomorrow, and forever.

A Parent Tip

Remember the good old days when parents demanded that their children be polite and respectful, especially to adults? For wise parents, those good old days are now.

LOST IN THE CROWD

The fear of human opinion disables; trusting in God protects you from that.

PROVERBS 29:25 MSG

Rick Warren observed, "Those who follow the crowd usually get lost in it." We know these words to be true, but oftentimes we fail to live by them. Instead of trusting God for guidance, we imitate our neighbors and suffer the consequences. Instead of seeking to please our Father in heaven, we strive to please our peers, with decidedly mixed results.

Whom will you try to please today: your God or your peers? Your family's obligation is most certainly not to neighbors or friends. Your obligation is to an all-knowing, all-powerful God. You must seek to please Him first and always. No exceptions.

A Talking Point

Today, talk to your daughter about the importance of pleasing God first and people next.

Day 118

FOOLISH PRIDE

Do nothing out of rivalry or conceit, but in humility consider others as more important than yourselves.

PHILIPPIANS 2:3 HCSB

Sometimes our faith is tested more by prosperity than by adversity. Why? Because in times of plenty, we are tempted to stick out our chests and say, "I did that." But nothing could be further from the truth. All of our blessings start and end with God, and whatever "it" is, He did it. And He deserves the credit.

Who are the greatest among us? Are they the proud and the powerful? Hardly. The greatest among us are the humble servants who care less for their own glory and more for God's glory. If we seek greatness in God's eyes, we must forever praise God's good works, not our own.

A Talking Point

Today, talk to your daughter about the dangers of pride.

SERVING OTHERS WITH LOVE

Whoever wants to become great among you must be your servant.

MATTHEW 20:26 HCSB

Jesus came to earth as a servant of man and the Savior of mankind. One way that we can demonstrate our love for the Savior is by obeying His commandment to serve one another.

Whom will you choose to serve today? Will you be a parent who cheerfully meets the needs of family and friends? And, will you meet those needs with love in your heart and encouragement on your lips? As you plan for the day ahead, remember that the needs are great and the workers are few. And remember that God is doing His very best to enlist able-bodied believers—like you.

A Parent Tip

Be expressive. Make certain that at your house, love is expressed and demonstrated many times each day. Little acts of consideration and kindness can make a big difference in the way that your child views the world.

SETBACKS

And my God shall supply all your need according to His riches in glory by Christ Jesus.

PHILIPPIANS 4:19 NKJV

All of us experience adversity, disappointments, and hardship. Sometimes we bring these hardships upon ourselves, and sometimes we are victimized by circumstances that we cannot control and cannot fully understand. As human beings with limited insight, we can never completely comprehend the will of our Father in Heaven. But as believers in a benevolent God, we must always trust His providence.

Have you been touched by personal tragedy that you did not deserve and cannot understand? If so, it's time to make peace with life. It's time to forgive others, and, if necessary, to forgive yourself. It's time to accept the unchangeable past, to embrace the priceless present, and to have faith in the promise of tomorrow. It's time to trust God completely. And it's time to reclaim the peace—His peace—that can and should be yours.

A Talking Point

Today, talk to your daughter about the need to accept the things she cannot change.

BEYOND WORRY

Jesus said, "Don't let your hearts be troubled. Trust in God, and trust in me."

JOHN 14:1 NCV

Because we are fallible human beings, we worry. Even though we, as Christians, have the promise of God's love and protection, we find ourselves fretting over the countless details of everyday life.

If you are like most parents, you may, on occasion, find yourself worrying about health, about finances, about safety, about relationships, about family, and about countless other challenges of life, some great and some small. Where is the best place to take your worries? Take them to God. Take your troubles to Him, and your fears, and your sorrows. And remember: God is trustworthy… and you are protected.

A Parent Tip

If you're worried about your future, your family, or anything else, for that matter, pray about it. God is bigger than your problems.

Day 122

IT'S UP TO YOU TO ASK

If you need wisdom—if you want to know what God wants you to do—ask him, and he will gladly tell you. He will not resent your asking.

JAMES 1:5 NLT

Jesus made it clear to His disciples: they should petition God to meet their needs. So should we. Genuine, heartfelt prayer produces powerful changes in us and in our world. When we lift our hearts to God, we open ourselves to a never-ending source of divine wisdom and infinite love.

Do you have questions about your future that you simply can't answer? Do you have needs that you simply can't meet by yourself? Do you sincerely seek to know God's unfolding plans for your life? If so, ask Him for direction, for protection, and for strength—and then keep asking Him every day that you live. Whatever your need, no matter how great or small, pray about it and never lose hope. God is not just near; He is here, and He's perfectly capable of answering your prayers. Now, it's up to you to ask.

A Talking Point

Today, talk to your son about the need to ask God for His guidance.

A PRICELESS GIFT

Man shall not live by bread alone, but by every word that proceeds from the mouth of God.

MATTHEW 4:4 NKJV

The Bible is a priceless gift, a tool for Christians to use as they share the Good News of their Savior, Christ Jesus. Too many Christians, however, keep their spiritual tool kits tightly closed and out of sight.

Jonathan Edwards advised, "Be assiduous in reading the Holy Scriptures. This is the fountain whence all knowledge in divinity must be derived. Therefore let not this treasure lie by you neglected."

God's Holy Word is, indeed, a priceless, one-of-a-kind treasure. Handle it with care, but more importantly, handle it every day . . . starting today.

A Parent Tip

You may have many books on your bookshelf, but the most important one BY FAR is the Holy Bible. So be sure to open your Bible early and often.

Day 124

BORN AGAIN

You have been born again, and this new life did not come from something that dies, but from something that cannot die. You were born again through God's living message that continues forever.

1 PETER 1:23 NCV

Why did Christ die on the cross? Christ sacrificed His life so that we might be born again. This gift, freely given from God's only begotten Son, is the priceless possession of everyone who accepts Him as Lord and Savior. Let us claim Christ's gift today. Let us walk with the Savior, let us love Him, let us praise Him, and let us share His message of salvation with all those who cross our paths.

The comforting words of Ephesians 2:8 make God's promise clear: "For by grace you have been saved through faith, and that not of yourselves; it is the gift of God" (NKJV). Thus, we are saved not because of our good deeds but because of our faith in Christ. May we, who have been given so much, praise our Savior for the gift of salvation, and may we share the joyous news of our Master's limitless love with our families, with our friends, and with the world.

A Talking Point

Today, remind your daughter that the very best moment to let Jesus rule her heart is always the present moment.

IN HIS IMAGE

So God created man in his own image, in the image of God he created him; male and female he created them.

GENESIS 1:27 NIV

What is your attitude today? Are you fearful or worried? Are you more concerned about pleasing other people than pleasing God? Are you bitter, confused, cynical, or pessimistic? If so, it's time to have a little chat with your Father in heaven.

God intends that your life be filled with spiritual abundance and joy—but God will not force His joy upon you—you must claim it for yourself. So do yourself and your family this favor: accept God's gifts with a smile on your face, a song on your lips, and joy in your heart. Think optimistically about yourself and your future. Give thanks to the One who has given you everything, and trust in your heart that He wants to give you so much more.

A Parent Tip

Parental attitudes are contagious, so be sure that your attitude is positive, optimistic, and reverent.

Day 126

THE GUIDEBOOK

Every part of Scripture is God-breathed and useful one way or another, showing us truth, exposing our rebellion, correcting our mistakes, training us to live God's way. Through the Word we are put together and shaped up for the tasks God has for us.

2 TIMOTHY 3:16-17 MSG

God has given us a guidebook for righteous living called the Holy Bible. It contains thorough instructions which, if followed, lead to fulfillment, righteousness, and salvation. God has given us the Bible for the purpose of knowing His promises, His power, His commandments, His wisdom, His love, and His Son. As we study God's teachings and apply them to our lives, we live by the Word that shall never pass away. Today, let us follow God's commandments, and let us conduct our lives in such a way that we might be shining examples to our families, and, most importantly, to those who have not yet found Christ.

A Parent Tip

Your daughter will learn about Jesus at church and, in some cases, at school. But, the ultimate responsibility for religious teachings should never be delegated to institutions outside the home. As a parent, you must teach your child about Jesus using both your words and by your actions.

A HELPING HAND

Then a Samaritan traveling down the road came to where the hurt man was. When he saw the man, he felt very sorry for him. The Samaritan went to him, poured olive oil and wine on his wounds, and bandaged them. Then he put the hurt man on his own donkey and took him to an inn where he cared for him.

LUKE 10:33-34 NCV

Sometimes we would like to help make the world a better place, but we're not sure how to do it. Jesus told the story of the "Good Samaritan," a man who helped a fellow traveler when no one else would. We, too, should be good Samaritans when we find people who need our help.

When bad things happen in our world, there's always something we can do. So what can you do to make God's world a better place? You can start by making your own corner of the world a little nicer place to live (by sharing kind words and good deeds). And then, you can take your concerns to God in prayer.

A Quote to Talk About

We can never untangle all the woes in other people's lives. We can't produce miracles overnight. But we can bring a cup of cool water to a thirsty soul, or a scoop of laughter to a lonely heart.

BARBARA JOHNSON

Day 128

TALK ABOUT SAFETY

A prudent person foresees the danger ahead and takes precautions. The simpleton goes blindly on and suffers the consequences.

PROVERBS 22:3 NLT

Since no one can deny that far too many young people behave recklessly, it's your job, as a responsible parent, to do everything within your power to ensure that your child is far more safety conscious than the norm. In short, you should become your family's safety advisor. You should be vocal, you should be persistent, you should be consistent, and you should be informed.

Maturity and safety go hand in hand. So, as your daughter becomes a more mature young woman, she'll naturally, if gradually, acquire the habit of looking before she leaps. And that's good because when young people leap first and look second, they often engage in destructive behavior that they soon come to regret.

A Talking Point

Today, talk to your daughter about slowing down, buckling up, thinking ahead, being smart, and staying safe.

OBEDIENCE NOW

And hereby we do know that we know him, if we keep his commandments.

1 JOHN 2:3 KJV

In order to enjoy a deeper relationship with God, you must strive diligently to live in accordance with His commandments. But there's a problem—you live in a world that seeks to snare your attention and lead you away from God.

Because you are an imperfect being, you cannot be perfectly obedient, nor does God expect you to be. What is required, however, is a sincere desire to be obedient coupled with an awareness of sin and a willingness to distance yourself from it as soon as you encounter it.

Are you willing to conform your behavior to God's rules? Hopefully, you can answer that question with a resounding yes. Otherwise, you'll never experience a full measure of the blessings that the Creator gives to those who obey Him.

A Parent Tip

Your attitude toward church will help determine your kid's attitude toward church . . . so celebrate accordingly!

Day 130

FEEDING THE CHURCH

God put everything under his power and made him the head over everything for the church, which is Christ's body. The church is filled with Christ, and Christ fills everything in every way.

EPHESIANS 1:22-23 NCV

In the Book of Acts, Luke reminds us to "feed the church of God" (20:28). As Christians who have been saved by a loving, compassionate Creator, we are compelled not only to worship Him in our hearts but also to worship Him in the presence of fellow believers.

Do you feed the church of God? Do you attend regularly, and are you an active participant? The answer to these questions will have a profound impact on the quality and direction of your spiritual journey.

So do yourself and your family a favor: become actively involved in your church. Don't just go to church out of habit. Go to church out of a sincere desire to know and worship God. When you do, you'll be blessed by the One who sent His Son to die so that you might have everlasting life.

A Parent Tip

Make church a celebration, not an obligation: What you put into church determines what you get out of it. Your attitude towards worship is vitally important . . . so celebrate accordingly!

OLD YOU, NEW YOU

Therefore, if anyone is in Christ, he is a new creation; old things have passed away; behold, all things have become new.

2 CORINTHIANS 5:17 NKJV

Think, for a moment, about the "old" you, the person you were before you invited Christ to reign over your heart. Now, think about the "new" you, the person you have become since then. Is there a difference between the "old" you and the "new and improved" version? There should be! And that difference should be noticeable not only to you but also to others.

The Bible clearly teaches that when we welcome Christ into our hearts, we become new creations through Him. Our challenge, of course, is to behave ourselves like new creations. When we do, God fills our hearts, He blesses our endeavors, and transforms our lives . . . forever.

A Talking Point

Today, remind your daughter that a true conversion experience results in transformation: a life transformed by Christ and a commitment to follow faithfully in His footsteps.

Day 132

LIFE'S MOUNTAINTOPS, LIFE'S VALLEYS

I sought the Lord, and He heard me, and delivered me from all my fears.

PSALM 34:4 NKJV

Every life (including yours) is an unfolding series of events: some fabulous, some not-so-fabulous, and some downright disheartening. When you reach the mountaintops of life, praising God is easy. But, when the storm clouds form overhead, your faith will be tested, sometimes to the breaking point. As a believer, you can take comfort in this fact: Wherever you find yourself, whether at the top of the mountain or the depths of the valley, God is there, and because He cares for you, you can live courageously.

The next time you find your courage tested to the limit, remember that God is your shield and your strength; He is your protector and your deliverer. Call upon Him in your hour of need and He will protect you.

A Parent Tip

When questions can be answered with a simple "yes" or "no," children will tend to answer accordingly; a better strategy is to ask questions that require a more thoughtful response. Such questions might begin with: "How do you feel about..." or "What do you think about...."

EXPECTING THE BEST

This is the day the Lord has made; let us rejoice and be glad in it.

PSALM 118:24 HCSB

What do you expect from the day ahead? Are you a parent who expects God to do wonderful things, or are you living beneath a cloud of apprehension and doubt? The familiar words of Psalm 118:24 remind us of a profound yet simple truth: "This is the day which the LORD hath made; we will rejoice and be glad in it" (KJV). For believers, every day begins and ends with God's Son and God's promises. When we accept Christ into our hearts, God promises us the opportunity for earthly peace and spiritual abundance. But more importantly, God promises us the priceless gift of eternal life.

As we face the inevitable challenges of life, we must arm ourselves with the promises of God's Holy Word. When we do, we can expect the best, not only for the day ahead, but also for all eternity.

A Parent Tip

Jesus came to life with a clear purpose: to save those who are lost. As a parent, it's up to you to make sure that your daughter understands why Jesus was born, why He lived, why He was crucified, and why He was resurrected.

Day 134

THE REMEDY FOR UNCERTAINTY

But He said to them, "Why are you fearful, you of little faith?" Then He got up and rebuked the winds and the sea. And there was a great calm.

MATTHEW 8:26 HCSB

Sometimes, like Jesus' disciples, we feel threatened by the storms of life. During these moments, when our hearts are flooded with uncertainty, we must remember that God is not simply near, He is here.

Have you ever felt your faith in God slipping away? If so, you are in good company. Even the most faithful Christians are, at times, beset by occasional bouts of discouragement and doubt. But even when you feel far removed from God, God never leaves your side. He is always with you, always willing to calm the storms of life. When you sincerely seek His presence—and when you genuinely seek to establish a deeper, more meaningful relationship with His Son—God will calm your fears, answer your prayers, and restore your soul.

A Quote to Talk About

Fear and doubt are conquered by a faith that rejoices. And faith can rejoice because the promises of God are as certain as God Himself.

KAY ARTHUR

SUFFICIENT FOR YOUR NEEDS

And God will generously provide all you need. Then you will always have everything you need and plenty left over to share with others.

2 CORINTHIANS 9:8 NLT

Of this you can be sure: the love of God is sufficient to meet your needs. Whatever dangers you may face, whatever heartbreaks you must endure, God is with you, and He stands ready to comfort you and to heal you.

The Psalmist writes, "Weeping may endure for a night, but joy comes in the morning" (Psalm 30:5 NKJV). But when we are suffering, the morning may seem very far away. It is not. God promises that He is "near to those who have a broken heart" (Psalm 34:18 NKJV).

If you are experiencing the intense pain of a recent loss, or if you are still mourning a loss from long ago, perhaps you are now ready to begin the next stage of your journey with God. If so, be mindful of this fact: the loving heart of God is sufficient to meet any challenge.

A Parent Tip

Make your home a gossip-free zone. Gossip is a learned behavior. Make sure that your kids don't learn it from you!

WHEN IT'S HARD TO BE KIND

Don't be obsessed with getting your own advantage. Forget yourselves long enough to lend a helping hand.

PHILIPPIANS 2:4 MSG

Sometimes, when we feel happy or generous, we find it easy to be kind. Other times, when we are discouraged or tired, we can scarcely summon the energy to utter a single kind word. But, God's commandment is clear: He intends that we make the conscious choice to treat others with kindness and respect, no matter our circumstances, no matter our emotions.

Today, as you consider all the things that Christ has done in your life, honor Him by following His commandment and obeying the Golden Rule. He expects no less, and He deserves no less.

A Parent Tip

The Golden Rule . . . is as good as gold—in fact, it's better than gold. And as a responsible parent, you should make certain that your child knows that the Golden Rule is, indeed, golden.

PRACTICING WHAT WE PREACH

If the way you live isn't consistent with what you believe, then it's wrong.

ROMANS 14:23 MSG

In describing our beliefs, our actions are far better descriptors than our words. Yet far too many of us spend more energy talking about our beliefs than living by them—with predictably poor results.

As believers, we must beware: Our actions should always give credence to the changes that Christ can make in the lives of those who walk with Him.

Your beliefs shape your values, and your values shape your life. Is your life a clearly-crafted picture book of your creed? Are your actions always consistent with your beliefs? Are you willing to practice the philosophies that you preach? Hopefully so; otherwise, you'll be tormented by inconsistencies between your beliefs and your behaviors.

A Parent Tip

Talking about your beliefs is easy. But, making your actions match your words is much harder. Nevertheless, if you really want to be honest with yourself and your family, then you must make your actions match your beliefs. Period.

Day 138

THE WISDOM TO BE HUMBLE

When you do things, do not let selfishness or pride be your guide. Instead, be humble and give more honor to others than to yourselves.

PHILIPPIANS 2:3 NCV

God's Word clearly instructs us to be humble. And that's good because, as fallible human beings, we have so very much to be humble about! Yet some of us continue to puff ourselves up, seeming to say, "Look at me!" To do so is wrong.

As Christians, we have been refashioned and saved by Jesus Christ, and that salvation came not because of our own good works but because of God's grace. How, then, can we be prideful? The answer, of course, is that, if we are honest with ourselves and with our God, we simply can't be boastful . . . we must, instead, be eternally grateful and exceedingly humble. The good things in our lives, including our loved ones, come from God. He deserves the credit—and we deserve the glorious experience of giving it to Him.

A Quote to Talk About

If you know who you are in Christ, your personal ego is not an issue.

BETH MOORE

BEING PATIENT WITH OURSELVES

Knowing God leads to self-control. Self-control leads to patient endurance, and patient endurance leads to godliness.

2 PETER 1:6 NLT

Being patient with other people can be difficult. But sometimes, we find it even more difficult to be patient with ourselves. We have high expectations and lofty goals. We want to accomplish things now, not later. And, of course, we want our lives to unfold according to our own timetables, not God's.

Throughout the Bible, we are instructed that patience is the companion of wisdom. God's message, then, is clear: we must be patient with all people, beginning with that particular person who stares back at us each time we gaze into the mirror.

A Parent Tip

From time to time, sit down and talk with your daughter about the images that she sees and the expectations she holds for herself. Remind your daughter that the Hollywood dream factory is not the real world.

Day 140

THE LOVE OF MONEY

For the love of money is a root of all sorts of evil, and some by longing for it have wandered away from the faith and pierced themselves with many griefs.

1 TIMOTHY 6:10 NASB

Our society is in love with money and the things that money can buy. God is not. God cares about people, not possessions, and so must we. We must, to the best of our abilities, love our neighbors as ourselves, and we must, to the best of our abilities, resist the mighty temptation to place possessions ahead of people.

Money, in and of itself, is not evil; worshipping money is. So today, as you prioritize matters of importance for you and yours, remember that God is almighty, but the dollar is not. If we worship God, we are blessed. But if we worship "the almighty dollar," we are inevitably punished because of our misplaced priorities—and our punishment usually comes sooner rather than later.

A Parent Tip

Corrie ten Boom observed, "I have held many things in my hands, and I have lost them all; but whatever I have placed in God's hands, that I still possess." Remember: your real riches are in heaven, so conduct yourself accordingly . . . and teach your children to do likewise.

LIFE'S FOUNDATION

The one who lives with integrity will be helped, but one who distorts right and wrong will suddenly fall.

PROVERBS 28:18 HCSB

Wise parents understand that character is a crucial building block in the foundation of a well-lived life. Character is built slowly over a lifetime. It is the sum of every right decision, every honest word, every noble thought, and every heartfelt prayer. It is forged on the anvil of honorable work and polished by the twin virtues of generosity and humility. Character is a precious thing—difficult to build, but easy to tear down; godly parents value it and protect it at all costs.

A Talking Point

Today, talk to your daughter about the rewards of honesty.

Day 142

ENDURING DIFFICULT DAYS

I have heard your prayer, I have seen your tears; behold, I will heal you....

2 KINGS 20:5 RSV

From time to time, all of us must endure discouragement and defeat. And, we sometimes experience life-changing personal losses that leave us reeling. When we do, God stands ready to protect us. When we are troubled, we must call upon God, and, in His own time and according to His own plan, He will heal us.

Are you an anxious parent? Take those anxieties to God. Are you troubled? Take your troubles to Him. Does your world seem to be trembling beneath your feet? Seek protection from the One who cannot be moved. The same God who created the universe will protect you if you ask Him...so ask Him.

A Talking Point

Today, remind your daughter that when she experiences tough times, she shouldn't keep her feelings bottled up inside. Instead, she should talk things over with you and with other people she trusts.

Day 143

SUPPORTING HIS CHURCH

For we are God's fellow workers; you are God's field, you are God's building.

1 CORINTHIANS 3:9 NKJV

The church belongs to God; it is His just as certainly as we are His. When we help build God's church, we bear witness to the changes that He has made in our lives.

Today and every day, let us worship God with grateful hearts and helping hands as we support the church that He has created. Let us witness to our friends, to our families, and to the world. When we do so, we bless others—and we are blessed by the One who sent His Son to die so that we might have eternal life.

A Parent Tip

Be an active participant at church. The church needs you and, just as importantly, you and your children need the church. So, don't hesitate to lean upon your church for support.

A CLEAR CONSCIENCE

Since, then, you have been raised with Christ, set your hearts on things above, where Christ is seated at the right hand of God. Set your minds on things above, not on earthly things.

COLOSSIANS 3:1-2 NIV

It's a fact: Few things in life torment us more than a guilty conscience. And, few things in life provide more contentment than the knowledge that we are obeying God's commandments.

A clear conscience is one of the rewards we earn when we obey God's Word and follow His will. When we follow God's will and accept His gift of salvation, our earthly rewards are never-ceasing, and our heavenly rewards are everlasting.

A Parent Tip

Sometimes, the little voice that we hear in our heads can be the echoes of our own parents' voices. Now that you're a parent, you're the one whose words will echo down through the hearts and minds of future generations. It's a big responsibility, but with God's help, you're up to the challenge.

THE MORNING WATCH

Morning by morning he wakens me and opens my understanding to his will. The Sovereign Lord has spoken to me, and I have listened.

ISAIAH 50:4-5 NLT

Each new day is a gift from God, and if you are wise, you will spend a few quiet moments each morning thanking the Giver. When you begin each day with your head bowed and your heart lifted, you are reminded of God's love, His protection, and His commandments. Then, you can align your priorities for the coming day with the teachings and commandments that God has placed upon your heart.

So, if you've acquired the unfortunate habit of trying to "squeeze" God into the corners of your life, it's time to reshuffle the items on your to-do list by placing God first. And if you haven't already done so, form the habit of spending quality time with your Father in heaven. He deserves it . . . and so do you.

A Parent Tip

God is available to you every morning . . . so you and your family members should make yourselves available to Him.

Day 146

WHEN PEOPLE MISBEHAVE

Bad temper is contagious—don't get infected.

PROVERBS 22:25 MSG

Face it: sometimes people can be rude . . . very rude. When other people are unkind to you, you may be tempted to strike back, either verbally or in some other way. Don't do it! Instead, remember that God corrects other people's behaviors in His own way, and He doesn't need your help (even if you're totally convinced that He does).

So, when other people behave cruelly, foolishly, or impulsively—as they will from time to time—don't be hotheaded. Instead, speak up for yourself as politely as you can, and walk away. Then, forgive everybody as quickly as you can, and leave the rest up to God.

A Parent Tip

We live in a world that often resembles a desert of cynicism and mistrust. Therefore, we must make our homes an oasis of optimism and faith.

TEACHING DISCIPLINE

The one who follows instruction is on the path to life, but the one who rejects correction goes astray.

PROVERBS 10:17 HCSB

Wise parents understand the importance of discipline. In Proverbs 28:19, God's message is clear: "He who works his land will have abundant food, but the one who chases fantasies will have his fill of poverty" (NIV). When we work diligently and consistently, we can expect a bountiful harvest. But we must never expect the harvest to precede the labor.

Thoughtful Christians understand that God doesn't reward laziness or misbehavior. To the contrary, God expects His children (of all ages) to lead disciplined lives . . . very disciplined lives.

A Parent Tip

Being a popular parent isn't nearly as important as being a godly parent. So, when there's a choice between pleasing your kids or pleasing your God, please God.

Day 148

HOPE IS CONTAGIOUS

Finally, all of you should be of one mind, full of sympathy toward each other, loving one another with tender hearts and humble minds.

1 PETER 3:8 NLT

One of the reasons that God placed you here on earth is so that you might become a beacon of encouragement to your family and to the world. As a faithful follower of the One from Galilee, you have every reason to be hopeful, and you have every reason to share your hopes with others. When you do, you will discover that hope, like other human emotions, is contagious.

As a follower of Christ, you are instructed to choose your words carefully so as to build others up through wholesome, honest encouragement (Ephesians 4:29). So look for the good in others and celebrate the good that you find. As the old saying goes, "When someone does something good, applaud—you'll make two people happy."

A Parent Tip

As a parent, it's up to you to establish the general tone of the conversations that occur in your home. Make certain that the tone you set is worthy of the One you worship.

A POSITIVE INFLUENCE

Be an example to the believers in word, in conduct, in love, in spirit, in faith, in purity.

1 TIMOTHY 4:12 NKJV

As followers of Christ, we must each ask ourselves an important question: "What kind of example am I?" The answer to that question determines, in large part, whether or not we are positive influences on our own little corners of the world.

Are you the kind of parent whose life serves as a powerful example of righteousness? Are you a person whose behavior serves as a positive role model for your children? Are you the kind of Christian whose actions, day in and day out, are based upon integrity, fidelity, and a love for the Lord? If so, you are not only blessed by God, you are also a powerful force for good in a world that desperately needs positive influences such as yours.

A Parent Tip

Parental pronouncements are easy to make but much harder to live by. But whether you like it or not, you are almost certainly the most important role model for your child. Behave accordingly.

Day 150

CARING FOR YOUR FAMILY

But if anyone does not provide for his own, and especially for those of his household, he has denied the faith and is worse than an unbeliever.

1 TIMOTHY 5:8 NASB

The words of 1 Timothy 5:8 are unambiguous: if God has blessed us with families, then He expects us to care for them. Sometimes, this profound responsibility seems daunting. And sometimes, even for the most dedicated Christian parents, family life holds moments of frustration and disappointment. But, for those who are lucky enough to live in the presence of a close-knit, caring clan, the rewards far outweigh the demands.

No family is perfect, and neither is yours. Despite the inevitable challenges of providing for your family, and despite the occasional hurt feelings of family life, your clan is God's gift to you. Give thanks to the Giver for the gift of family . . . and act accordingly.

A Parent Tip

Your children deserve to grow up in a happy home. As a parent, you owe it to them (and to yourself) to provide that kind of home.

PASS IT ON

Do not neglect the spiritual gift that is within you....

1 TIMOTHY 4:14 NASB

God has given you an array of talents, and He has given you unique opportunities to share those talents with the world. Your Creator intends for you to use your talents for the glory of His kingdom in the service of His children. Will you honor Him by sharing His gifts? And, will you share His gifts humbly and lovingly? Hopefully you will.

The old saying is both familiar and true: "What you are is God's gift to you; what you become is your gift to God." As a believer who has been touched by the transforming love of Jesus Christ, your obligation is clear: You must strive to make the most of your own God-given talents, and you must encourage your family members to do likewise. So, make this promise to yourself and to God: Promise to use your talents to minister to your family, to your friends, and to the world. And remember: The best way to say "Thank You" for God's gifts is to use them.

A Quote to Talk About

Not everyone possesses boundless energy or a conspicuous talent. We are not equally blessed with great intellect or physical beauty or emotional strength. But we have all been given the same ability to be faithful.

GIGI GRAHAM TCHIVIDJIAN

Day 152

LETTING GO

Blessed are the merciful, because they will be shown mercy.

MATTHEW 5:7 HCSB

Even the most mild-mannered parents will, on occasion, have reason to become angry with the inevitable shortcomings of family members and friends. But wise parents are quick to forgive others, just as God has forgiven them. The commandment to forgive others is clearly a part of God's Word, but oh how difficult a commandment it can be to follow. Because we are imperfect beings, we are quick to anger, quick to blame, slow to forgive, and even slower to forget. No matter. Even when forgiveness is difficult, God's instructions are straightforward: As Christians who have received the gift of forgiveness, we must now share that gift with others.

Bitterness and regret are not part of God's plan for your life. Forgiveness is. And once you've forgiven others, you can then turn your thoughts to a far more pleasant subject: the incredibly bright future that God has promised.

A Quote to Talk About

God expects us to forgive others as He has forgiven us; we are to follow His example by having a forgiving heart.

VONETTE BRIGHT

RICHLY BLESSED

God loves a cheerful giver.

2 CORINTHIANS 9:7 NIV

God's Word commands us to be generous, compassionate servants to those who need our support. As believers, we have been richly blessed by our Creator. We, in turn, are called to share our gifts, our possessions, our testimonies, and our talents.

The theme of generosity is one of the cornerstones of Christ's teachings. If we are to be disciples of Christ, we, too, must be cheerful, generous, courageous givers. Our Savior expects no less from us. And He deserves no less.

A Parent Tip

Being kind is a learned behavior. You're the teacher. Class is in session. Your child is in attendance. Actions speak louder than words. And it's one of the most important courses you will ever teach.

Day 154

BLESSED BEYOND MEASURE

The Lord bless you and keep you; the Lord make His face shine upon you, and be gracious to you.

NUMBERS 6:24-25 NKJV

Have you counted your blessings lately? You should. Of course, God's gifts are too numerous to count, but as a grateful Christian parent, you should attempt to count them nonetheless. Your blessings include life, family, friends, talents, and possessions, for starters. And your greatest gift—a treasure that was paid for on the cross and is yours for the asking—is God's gift of salvation through Christ Jesus.

As believing Christians, we have all been blessed beyond measure. Thus, thanksgiving should become a habit, a regular part of our daily routines. Today, let us pause and thank our Creator for His blessings. And let us demonstrate our gratitude to the Giver of all things good by using His gifts for the glory of His kingdom.

A Quote to Talk About

The Christian life is motivated, not by a list of do's and don'ts, but by the gracious outpouring of God's love and blessing.

ANNE GRAHAM LOTZ

GOD IS LOVE

My beloved friends, let us continue to love each other since love comes from God. Everyone who loves is born of God and experiences a relationship with God. The person who refuses to love doesn't know the first thing about God, because God is love—so you can't know him if you don't love.

1 JOHN 4:8 MSG

God loves you. He loves you more than you can imagine; His affection is deeper than you can fathom. God made you in His own image and gave you salvation through the person of His Son Jesus Christ. And as a result, you have an important decision to make.

When you accept the love that flows from the heart of God, you are transformed. When you embrace God's love, you feel differently about yourself, your neighbors, your community, your church, and your world. When you open your heart to God's love, you will feel compelled to share God's message—and His compassion—with others.

A Parent Tip

Remember that God's love doesn't simply flow to your children . . . it flows to you, too. And because God loves you, you can be certain that you, like your child, are wonderfully made and amazingly blessed.

Day 156

CONQUERING OUR FRUSTRATIONS

People with quick tempers cause trouble, but those who control their tempers stop a quarrel.

PROVERBS 15:18 NCV

Life is full of frustrations: some great and some small. On occasion, you, like Jesus, will confront evil, and when you do, you may respond as He did: vigorously and without reservation. But, more often your frustrations will be of the more mundane variety. As long as you live here on earth, you will face countless opportunities to lose your temper over small, relatively insignificant events: a traffic jam, a spilled cup of coffee, an inconsiderate comment, a broken promise.

When you are tempted to lose your temper over the minor inconveniences of life, don't. Turn away from anger, hatred, bitterness, and regret. Turn instead to God. When you do, you'll be following His commandments and giving yourself a priceless gift . . . the gift of peace.

A Parent Tip

When your daughter becomes angry or upset, you'll tend to become angry and upset, too. Resist that temptation. As the grown-up person in the family, it's up to you to remain calm, even when other, less mature members of the family can't.

GLORIOUS OPPORTUNITIES

Make the most of every opportunity.

COLOSSIANS 4:5 NIV

Are you a parent who is excited about the opportunities of today and thrilled by the possibilities of tomorrow? Do you confidently expect God to lead you to a place of abundance, peace, and joy? And, when your days on earth are over, do you expect to receive the priceless gift of eternal life? If you trust God's promises, and if you have welcomed God's Son into your heart, then you believe that your future is intensely and eternally bright.

Today, as you prepare to meet the duties of everyday life, pause and consider God's promises. And then think for a moment about the wonderful future that awaits all believers, including you. God has promised that your future is secure. Trust that promise, and celebrate the life of abundance and eternal joy that is now yours through Christ.

A Quote to Talk About

Lovely, complicated wrappings / Sheath the gift of one-day-more; / Breathless, I untie the package— / Never lived this day before!

GLORIA GAITHER

Day 158

THE POWER OF PERSEVERANCE

I do not consider myself to have taken hold of it. But one thing I do: forgetting what is behind and reaching forward to what is ahead, I pursue as my goal the prize promised by God's heavenly call in Christ Jesus.

PHILIPPIANS 3:13-14 HCSB

A well-lived life calls for preparation, determination, and, of course, lots of perseverance. As an example of perfect perseverance, we Christians need to look no further than our Savior, Jesus Christ. Jesus finished what He began. Despite His suffering, despite the shame of the cross, Jesus was steadfast in His faithfulness to God. We, too, must remain faithful, especially during times of hardship. Sometimes, God may answer our prayers with silence, and when He does, we must patiently persevere.

Are you facing a tough situation? If so, remember this: whatever your problem, God can handle it. Your job is to keep persevering until He does.

A Parent Tip

You will encounter occasional disappointments or failures. So will your children. But, don't invest large quantities of your life focusing on past misfortunes. Instead, look to the future with optimism and hope . . . and encourage your children to do the same.

FIRST THINGS FIRST

And I pray this: that your love will keep on growing in knowledge and every kind of discernment, so that you can determine what really matters and can be pure and blameless in the day of Christ.

PHILIPPIANS 1:9 HCSB

Have you fervently asked God to help prioritize your life? Have you asked Him for guidance and for the courage to do the things that you know need to be done? If so, then you're continually inviting your Creator to reveal Himself in a variety of ways. As a follower of Christ, you must do no less.

When you make God a full partner in every aspect of your life, He will lead you along the proper path: His path. When you allow God to reign over your heart, He will honor you with spiritual blessings that are simply too numerous to count. So, as you plan for the day ahead, make God's will your ultimate priority. When you do, your daily to-do list will take care of itself.

A Parent Tip

If your family is like most American families, you watch far too much television. And to make matters worse, some of the most popular shows are, at best, a waste of time and, at worst, a powerful negative influence on your family. So try this experiment: turn off all the televisions in your house at least one night a week.

Day 160

BEING GENTLE WITH YOURSELF

You're blessed when you're content with just who you are—no more, no less. That's the moment you find yourselves proud owners of everything that can't be bought.

MATTHEW 5:5 MSG

Being patient with ourselves can be difficult. We have high expectations and lofty goals. We want to receive God's blessings now, not later. We want our lives to unfold according to our own wishes and our own timetables—not God's. Yet throughout the Bible, we are instructed that patience is the companion of wisdom. Proverbs 16:32 teaches us that "Patience is better than strength" (NCV). God's message, then, is clear: we must be patient with all people, beginning with that particular person who stares back at us each time we gaze into the mirror.

Furthermore, the Bible teaches that when we genuinely open our hearts to Him, God accepts us just as we are. And, if He accepts us—faults and all—then who are we to believe otherwise?

A Quote to Talk About

May God help us to express and define ourselves in our one-of-a-kind way.

LUCI SWINDOLL

SERENITY

Do not remember the past events, pay no attention to things of old. Look, I am about to do something new; even now it is coming. Do you not see it? Indeed, I will make a way in the wilderness, rivers in the desert.

ISAIAH 43:18-19 HCSB

The American theologian Reinhold Niebuhr composed a profoundly simple verse that came to be known as the Serenity Prayer: "God, grant me the serenity to accept the things I cannot change, the courage to change the things I can, and the wisdom to know the difference." Niebuhr's words are far easier to recite than they are to live by. Why? Because most of us want life to unfold in accordance with our own wishes and timetables. But sometimes God has other plans.

If you've encountered unfortunate circumstances that are beyond your power to control, accept those circumstances . . . and trust God. When you do, you can be comforted in the knowledge that your Creator is both loving and wise, and that He understands His plans perfectly, even when you do not.

A Talking Point

Today, talk to your daughter about the need to trust God, especially when times are tough.

Day 162

THANKSGIVING YES . . . ENVY NO!

Stop your anger! Turn from your rage! Do not envy others—it only leads to harm.

PSALM 37:8 NLT

As the recipient of God's grace, you have every reason to celebrate life. After all, God has promised you the opportunity to receive His abundance and His joy—in fact, you have the opportunity to receive those gifts right now. But if you allow envy to gnaw away at the fabric of your soul, you'll find that joy remains elusive. So do yourself an enormous favor: Rather than succumbing to the sin of envy, focus on the marvelous things that God has done for you—starting with Christ's sacrifice. Thank the Giver of all good gifts, and keep thanking Him for the wonders of His love and the miracles of His creation. Count your own blessings and let your neighbors count theirs. It's the godly way to live.

A Talking Point

Today, talk to your daughter about the futility of envy.

TREAT THE MEDIA WITH CAUTION

Be careful! Watch out for attacks from the Devil, your great enemy. He prowls around like a roaring lion, looking for some victim to devour. Take a firm stand against him, and be strong in your faith.

1 PETER 5:8-9 NLT

The media is working around the clock in an attempt to rearrange your family's priorities in ways that are definitely not in your best interests. The media is trying to teach your family that physical appearance is all-important, that material possessions should be acquired at any cost, and that the world operates independently of God's laws. But guess what? Those messages are lies.

Will you control what appears on your TV screen, or will you be controlled by it? If you're willing to take complete control over the images that appear inside the four walls of your home, you'll be doing yourselves a king-sized favor. So forget the media hype, and pay attention to God. Stand up for Him and be counted, not just in church where it's relatively easy to be a Christian, but also when you're deciding what to watch.

A Parent Tip

As a parent, you are the person in charge of deciding what media is appropriate for your family. Choose wisely.

GOD'S PLAN FOR YOUR FAMILY

Unless the Lord builds a house, its builders labor over it in vain; unless the Lord watches over a city, the watchman stays alert in vain.

PSALM 127:1 HSCB

As you consider God's purpose for your own life, you must also consider how your plans will effect the most important people that God has entrusted to your care: your loved ones.

A loving family is a treasure from God. If you happen to be a member of a close knit, supportive clan, offer a word of thanks to your Creator. He has blessed you with one of His most precious earthly possessions. Your obligation, in response to God's gift, is to treat your family in ways that are consistent with His commandments. So, as you prayerfully seek God's direction, remember that He has important plans for your home life as well as your professional life. It's up to you to act—and to plan—accordingly.

A Quote to Talk About

The Golden Rule begins at home.

MARIE T. FREEMAN

OUR FEAR-BASED WORLD

They do not fear bad news; they confidently trust the Lord to care for them. They are confident and fearless and can face their foes triumphantly.

PSALM 112:7-8 NLT

We live in a fear-based world, a world where bad new travels at light speed and good news doesn't. These are troubled times, times when we have legitimate fears for the future of our nation, our world, and our families. But as Christians, we have every reason to live courageously. After all, the ultimate battle has already been fought and won on that faraway cross at Calvary.

Perhaps you, like countless other parents, have found your courage tested by the anxieties and fears that are an inevitable part of life. If so, God wants to have a little chat with you. The next time you find your courage tested to the limit, God wants to remind you that He is not just near, He is here. So remember this: your Heavenly Father is your Protector and your Deliverer. Call upon Him in your hour of need, and be comforted. Whatever your challenge, God can handle it. And will.

A Quote to Talk About

Whether our fear is absolutely realistic or out of proportion in our minds, our greatest refuge is Jesus Christ.

LUCI SWINDOLL

Day 166

A WILLINGNESS TO FORGIVE

Be kind to each other, tenderhearted, forgiving one another, just as God through Christ has forgiven you.

EPHESIANS 4:32 NLT

To forgive others is difficult. Being frail, fallible, imperfect human beings, we are quick to anger, quick to blame, slow to forgive, and even slower to forget. No matter. Forgiveness, no matter how difficult, is God's way, and it must be our way, too.

God's commandments are not intended to be customized for the particular whims of particular believers. God's Word is not a menu from which each of us may select items á la carte, according to our own desires. Far from it. God's Holy Word is a book that must be taken in its entirety; all of God's commandments are to be taken seriously. And, so it is with forgiveness. So, if you hold bitterness against even a single person, forgive. Then, to the best of your abilities, forget. It's God's way for you to live.

A Parent Tip

Teach the importance of forgiveness every day, and, if necessary, use words.

FINDING FULFILLMENT

For You, O God, have tested us; You have refined us as silver is refined . . . we went through fire and through water; but You brought us out to rich fulfillment.

PSALM 66:10–12 NKJV

Everywhere we turn, or so it seems, the world promises fulfillment, contentment, and happiness. But the contentment that the world offers is fleeting and incomplete. Thankfully, the fulfillment that God offers is all encompassing and everlasting.

Sometimes, amid the inevitable hustle and bustle of life, we can forfeit—albeit temporarily—the joy of Christ as we wrestle with the challenges of daily living. Yet God's Word is clear: fulfillment through Christ is available to all who seek it and claim it. Count yourself among that number. Seek first a personal, transforming relationship with Jesus, and then claim the joy, the fulfillment, and the spiritual abundance that the Shepherd offers His sheep.

A Talking Point

Today, talk to your daughter about ways she can find lasting fulfillment.

Day 168

HIS GENEROSITY . . . AND YOURS

But God proves His own love for us in that while we were still sinners Christ died for us!

ROMANS 5:8 HCSB

Christ showed His love for us by willingly sacrificing His own life so that we might have eternal life. We, as Christ's followers, are challenged to share His love. And, when we walk each day with Jesus—and obey the commandments found in God's Holy Word—we are worthy ambassadors for Him.

Just as Christ has been—and will always be—the ultimate friend to His flock, so should we be Christlike in our love and generosity to those in need. When we share the love of Christ, we share a priceless gift. As His servants, we must do no less.

A Parent Tip

God has given your family countless blessings, and He wants you and your kids to share those blessings generously, humbly, and often.

AT PEACE WITH YOUR PAST

Forget about what's happened; don't keep going over old history. Be alert, be present. I'm about to do something brand-new. It's bursting out! Don't you see it? There it is! I'm making a road through the desert, rivers in the badlands.

ISAIAH 43:18–19 MSG

Have you made peace with your past? If so, congratulations. But, if you are mired in the quicksand of regret, it's time to plan your escape. How can you do so? By accepting what has been and by trusting God for what will be.

Because you are human, you may be slow to forget yesterday's disappointments. But, if you sincerely seek to focus your hopes and energies on the future, then you must find ways to accept the past, no matter how difficult it may be to do so. So, if you have not yet made peace with the past, today is the day to declare an end to all hostilities. When you do, you can then turn your thoughts to wondrous promises of God and to the glorious future that He has in store for you.

A Parent Tip

No parent is perfect, not even you. Consequently, you will make mistakes from time to time (and yes, you might even lose your temper). When you make a mistake, apologize to the offended party, especially if that party is related to you by birth.

Day 170

THE CHAINS OF PERFECTIONISM

Those who wait for perfect weather will never plant seeds; those who look at every cloud will never harvest crops.

ECCLESIASTES 11:4 NCV

The media delivers an endless stream of messages that tell you and your family members how to look, how to behave, and how to dress. The media's expectations are impossible to meet—God's are not. God doesn't expect perfection . . . and neither should you.

If you find yourself bound up by the chains of perfectionism, it's time to ask yourself who you're trying to impress, and why. If you're trying to impress other people, it's time to reconsider your priorities. Your first responsibility is to the Heavenly Father who created you and to His Son who saved you. Then, you bear a powerful responsibility to your family. But, when it comes to meeting society's unrealistic expectations, forget it! After all, pleasing God is simply a matter of obeying His commandments and accepting His Son. But as for pleasing everybody else? That's impossible!

A Talking Point

Today, talk to your daughter about the dangers of perfectionism.

SOLVING PROBLEMS

People who do what is right may have many problems, but the Lord will solve them all.

PSALM 34:19 NCV

Life is an exercise in problem-solving. The question is not whether we will encounter problems; the real question is how we will choose to address them. When it comes to solving the problems of everyday living, we often know precisely what needs to be done, but we may be slow in doing it—especially if what needs to be done is difficult or uncomfortable for us. So we put off till tomorrow what should be done today.

The words of Psalm 34 remind us that the Lord solves problems for "people who do what is right." And usually, doing "what is right" means doing the uncomfortable work of confronting our problems sooner rather than later. So with no further ado, let the problem-solving begin . . . now.

A Parent Tip

If you tend to overestimate your problems and under count your blessings, your kids will, too. But if you assess your problems realistically and seek the Lord's help in solving them, your children will learn that no problem is too big for God.

Day 172

THE SIMPLE LIFE

Whoever becomes simple and elemental again, like this child, will rank high in God's kingdom.

MATTHEW 18:4 MSG

You and your family live in a world where simplicity is in short supply. Think for a moment about the complexity of your every-day life and compare it to the lives of your ancestors. Certainly, you are the beneficiary of many technological innovations, but those innovations have a price: in all likelihood, your world is highly complex.

Unless you take firm control of your time and your life, you may be overwhelmed by an ever-increasing tidal wave of complexity that threatens your happiness. But your Heavenly Father understands the joy of living simply, and so should you. So do yourself a favor: keep your life as simple as possible. Simplicity is, indeed, genius. By simplifying your life, you are destined to improve it.

A Quote to Talk About

Nobody is going to simplify your life for you. You've got to simplify things for yourself.

MARIE T. FREEMAN

SHOUT FOR JOY

Shout triumphantly to the Lord, all the earth. Serve the Lord with gladness; come before Him with joyful songs.

PSALM 100:1-2 HCSB

The 100th Psalm reminds us that the entire earth should "Shout for joy to the Lord." As God's children, we are blessed beyond measure, but sometimes, as busy parents struggling to raise our children in a difficult world, we neglect to count our blessings.

Our blessings include life and health, family and friends, freedom and possessions—for starters. And, the gifts we receive from God are multiplied when we share them. May we always give thanks to God for His blessings, and may we always demonstrate our gratitude by sharing our gifts with others. The 118th Psalm reminds us that, "This is the day which the LORD has made; let us rejoice and be glad in it" (v. 24, NASB). May we celebrate this day and the One who created it.

A Parent Tip

God has given you the gift of life (here on earth) and the promise of eternal life (in heaven). Now, He wants you to celebrate those gifts with your family.

Day 174

TURNING AWAY FROM ANGER

My dear brothers and sisters, always be willing to listen and slow to speak. Do not become angry easily, because anger will not help you live the right kind of life God wants.

JAMES 1:19-20 NCV

Perhaps God gave each of us one mouth and two ears in order that we might listen twice as much as we speak. Unfortunately, many of us do otherwise, especially when we become angry.

Anger is a natural human emotion that is sometimes necessary and appropriate. Even Jesus Himself became angered when He confronted the moneychangers in the temple. But, more often than not, our frustrations are of the more mundane variety. When you are tempted to lose your temper over the minor inconveniences of life, don't. Turn away from anger, and turn instead to God.

A Parent Tip

If you expect your child to control her temper—and you should—then you, as the adult in the family, must also control yours.

FEARING GOD

The fear of the Lord is the beginning of knowledge.

PROVERBS 1:7 HCSB

Are you a parent who possesses a healthy, fearful respect for God's power? Hopefully so. After all, God's Word teaches that the fear of the Lord is the beginning of knowledge (Proverbs 1:7).

When we fear the Creator—and when we honor Him by obeying His commandments—we receive God's approval and His blessings. But, when we ignore Him or disobey His commandments, we invite disastrous consequences. God's hand shapes the universe, and it shapes our lives. As believers, we must cultivate a sincere respect for God's awesome power. The fear of the Lord is, indeed, the beginning of knowledge. So today, as you face the realities of everyday life, remember this: until you acquire a healthy, respectful fear of God's power, your education is incomplete, and so is your faith.

A Quote to Talk About

Spiritual worship comes from our very core and is fueled by an awesome reverence and desire for God.

BETH MOORE

Day 176

NOURISHED BY THE WORD

You will be a good servant of Christ Jesus, constantly nourished on the words of the faith and of the sound doctrine which you have been following.

1 TIMOTHY 4:6 NASB

Do you read your Bible a lot . . . or not? The answer to this simple question will determine, to a surprising extent, the quality of your life and the direction of your faith.

As you establish priorities for life, you must decide whether God's Word will be a bright spotlight that guides your path every day or a tiny nightlight that occasionally flickers in the dark. The decision to study the Bible—or not—is yours and yours alone. But make no mistake: how you choose to use your Bible will have a profound impact on you and your loved ones.

The Bible is the ultimate guide for life; make it your family's guidebook as well. When you do, you can be comforted in the knowledge that your steps are guided by a Source of wisdom and truth that never fails.

A Talking Point

Today, remind your daughter that nobody can study the Bible for her . . . she's got to study it for herself. And that's exactly what she should do.

TOO BUSY

Careful planning puts you ahead in the long run; hurry and scurry puts you further behind.

PROVERBS 21:5 MSG

If you're a parent with too many responsibilities and too few hours in which to fulfill them, you are not alone. The job of parenting can be so demanding that sometimes you may feel as if you have no time for yourself . . . and no time for God.

Has the busy pace of life robbed you of the peace that might otherwise be yours through Jesus Christ? If so, you are simply too busy for your own good. Through His Son Jesus, God offers you a peace that passes human understanding, but He won't force His peace upon you; in order to experience it, you must slow down long enough to sense His presence and His love.

Today, as a gift to yourself, to your family, and to the world, slow down long enough to claim the inner peace that is your spiritual birthright: the peace of Jesus Christ. It is offered freely; it has been paid for in full; it is yours for the asking. So ask. And then share.

A Parent Tip

The world wants to grab every spare minute of your time, but God wants some of your time, too. When in doubt, trust God.

Day 178

THE GIFT OF CHEERFULNESS

Worry is a heavy load, but a kind word cheers you up.

PROVERBS 12:25 NCV

Cheerfulness is a gift that we give to others and to ourselves. And, as believers who have been saved by a risen Christ, why shouldn't we be cheerful? The answer, of course, is that we have every reason to honor our Savior with joy in our hearts, smiles on our faces, and words of celebration on our lips.

Christ promises us lives of abundance and joy if we accept His love and His grace. Yet sometimes, even the most righteous among us are beset by fits of ill temper and frustration. During these moments, we may not feel like turning our thoughts and prayers to Christ, but that's precisely what we should do. When we do so, we simply can't stay grumpy for long.

A Parent Tip

Cheerfulness is an attitude that is highly contagious. Kids often catch it from their parents. Remember that cheerfulness starts at the top. A cheerful household usually begins with cheerful adults.

A GROWING RELATIONSHIP WITH GOD

Grow in grace and understanding of our Master and Savior, Jesus Christ. Glory to the Master, now and forever! Yes!

2 PETER 3:18 MSG

Your relationship with God is ongoing; it unfolds day by day, and it offers countless opportunities to grow closer to Him . . . or not. As each new day unfolds, you are confronted with a wide range of decisions: how you will behave, where you will direct your thoughts, with whom you will associate, and what you will choose to worship. These choices, along with many others like them, are yours and yours alone. How you choose determines how your relationship with God will unfold.

Are you continuing to grow in your love and knowledge of the Lord, or are you "satisfied" with the current state of your spiritual health? Hopefully, you're determined to make yourself a growing Christian. Your Savior deserves no less, and neither, by the way, do you.

A Parent Tip

Be an active participant at church: the church needs you and, just as importantly, you and your children need the church. So, don't hesitate to lean upon your church for support.

Day 180

HIS COMFORTING HAND

God, who comforts the downcast, comforted us....

2 CORINTHIANS 7:6 NIV

If you have been touched by the transforming hand of Jesus, then you have every reason to live courageously. Still, even if you are a dedicated Christian, you may find yourself discouraged by the inevitable disappointments and tragedies that occur in the lives of believers and non-believers alike.

The next time you find your courage tested to the limit, lean upon God's promises. Trust His Son. Remember that God is always near and that He is your protector and your deliverer. When you are worried, anxious, or afraid, call upon Him and accept the touch of His comforting hand. Remember that God rules both mountaintops and valleys—with limitless wisdom and love—now and forever.

A Quote to Talk About

Put your hand into the hand of God. He gives the calmness and serenity of heart and soul.

MRS. CHARLES E. COWMAN

DISCOVERING GOD'S PLANS

For it is God who is working among you both the willing and the working for His good purpose.

PHILIPPIANS 2:13 HCSB

If you seek to live in accordance with God's will for your life—and you should—then you will live in accordance with His commandments. You will study God's Word, and you will be watchful for His signs. You will associate with fellow Christians who will encourage your spiritual growth, and you will listen to that inner voice that speaks to you in the quiet moments of your daily devotionals.

God intends to use you in wonderful, unexpected ways if you let Him. The decision to seek God's plan and to follow it is yours and yours alone. The consequences of that decision have implications that are both profound and eternal, so choose carefully.

A Talking Point

Today, talk to your daughter about the need to study God's Word and follow God's plan.

Day 182

STRENGTH FOR TODAY

I can do all things through Christ which strengtheneth me.

PHILIPPIANS 4:13 KJV

Have you made God the cornerstone of your life, or is He relegated to a few hours on Sunday morning? Have you genuinely allowed God to reign over every corner of your heart, or have you attempted to place Him in a spiritual compartment? The answer to these questions will determine the direction of your day and your life.

God loves you. In times of trouble, He will comfort you; in times of sorrow, He will dry your tears. When you are weak or sorrowful, God is as near as your next breath. He stands at the door of your heart and waits. Welcome Him in and allow Him to rule. And then, accept the peace, and the strength, and the protection, and the abundance that only God can give.

A Quote to Talk About

In my weakness, I have learned, like Moses, to lean hard on God. The weaker I am, the harder I lean on Him. The harder I lean, the stronger I discover Him to be. The stronger I discover God to be, the more resolute I am in this job He's given me to do.

JONI EARECKSON TADA

LIGHTING THE PATH

Your word is a lamp to my feet and a light to my path.

PSALM 119:105 NKJV

Are you a parent who trusts God's Word without reservation? Hopefully so, because the Bible is unlike any other book—it is a guidebook for life here on earth and for life eternal. The Psalmist describes God's Word as, "a light to my path." Is the Bible your lamp? If not, you are depriving yourself of a priceless gift from the Creator.

Vance Havner observed, "It takes calm, thoughtful, prayerful meditation on the Word to extract its deepest nourishment." How true. God's Word can be a roadmap to a place of righteousness and abundance. Make it your roadmap. God's wisdom can be a light to guide your steps. Claim it as your light today, tomorrow, and every day of your life—and then walk confidently in the footsteps of God's only begotten Son.

A Quote to Talk About

If we neglect the Bible, we cannot expect to benefit from the wisdom and direction that result from knowing God's Word.

VONETTE BRIGHT

Day 184

NEIGHBORS IN NEED

Each one of us needs to look after the good of the people around us, asking ourselves, "How can I help?" That's exactly what Jesus did.

ROMANS 15:2-3 MSG

Neighbors. We know that we are instructed to love them, and yet there's so little time…and we're so busy. No matter. As Christians, we are commanded by our Lord and Savior Jesus Christ to love our neighbors just as we love ourselves. Period.

This very day, you will encounter someone who needs a word of encouragement, or a pat on the back, or a helping hand, or a heartfelt prayer. And, if you don't reach out to your friend, who will? If you don't take the time to understand the needs of your neighbors, who will? If you don't love your brothers and sisters, who will? So, today, look for a neighbor in need…and then do something to help. Father's orders.

A Talking Point

Today, talk to your daughter about what it means to be a good neighbor.

OFFERING THANKS

Give thanks in all circumstances; for this is God's will for you in Christ Jesus.

1 THESSALONIANS 5:18 NIV

Sometimes, life can be complicated, demanding, and frustrating. When the demands of life leave us rushing from place to place with scarcely a moment to spare, we may fail to pause and thank our Creator for His gifts. But, whenever we neglect to give proper thanks to the Father, we suffer because of our misplaced priorities.

Today, begin making a list of your blessings. You most certainly will not be able to make a complete list, but take a few moments and jot down as many blessings as you can. Then, give thanks to the Giver of all good things: God. His love for you is eternal, as are His gifts. And it's never too soon—or too late—to offer Him thanks.

A Quote to Talk About

When you and I are related to Jesus Christ, our strength and wisdom and peace and joy and love and hope may run out, but His life rushes in to keep us filled to the brim. We are showered with blessings, not because of anything we have or have not done, but simply because of Him.

ANNE GRAHAM LOTZ

Day 186

HIS AWESOME CREATION

Then God saw everything that He had made, and indeed it was very good.

GENESIS 1:31 NKJV

When we consider God's glorious universe, we marvel at the miracle of nature. The smallest seedlings and grandest stars are all part of God's infinite creation. God has placed His handiwork on display for all to see, and if we are wise, we will make time each day to celebrate the world that surrounds us.

Today, as you fulfill the demands of everyday life, pause to consider the majesty of heaven and earth. It is as miraculous as it is beautiful, as incomprehensible as it is breathtaking.

The Psalmist reminds us that the heavens are a declaration of God's glory (Psalm 19:1). May we never cease to praise the Father for a universe that stands as an awesome testimony to His presence and His power.

A Quote to Talk About

How awesome that the "Word" that was in the beginning, by which and through which God created everything, was—and is—a living Person with a mind, will, emotions, and intellect.

ANNE GRAHAM LOTZ

HIS INTIMATE LOVE

I've loved you the way my Father has loved me. Make yourselves at home in my love.

JOHN 15:9 MSG

St. Augustine observed, "God loves each of us as if there were only one of us." Do you believe those words? Do you seek an intimate, one-on-one relationship with your Heavenly Father, or are you satisfied to keep Him at a "safe" distance?

Sometimes, in the crush of our daily parental duties, God may seem far away, but He is not. God is everywhere we have ever been and everywhere we will ever go. He is with us night and day; He knows our thoughts and our prayers. And, when we earnestly seek Him, we will find Him because He is here, waiting patiently for us to reach out to Him. May we reach out to Him today and always. And may we praise Him for the glorious gifts that have transformed us today and forever.

A Parent Tip

You know that "God is love." Now, it's your responsibility to make certain that your children know it, too.

Day 188

HE REIGNS

In all your ways acknowledge Him, and He shall direct your paths.

PROVERBS 3:6 NKJV

God is sovereign. He reigns over the entire universe and He reigns over your little corner of that universe. Your challenge is to recognize God's sovereignty and live in accordance with His commandments. Sometimes, of course, this is easier said than done.

Your Heavenly Father may not always reveal Himself as quickly (or as clearly) as you would like. But rest assured: God is in control, God is here, and God intends to use you in wonderful, unexpected ways. He desires to lead you along a path of His choosing. Your challenge is to watch, to listen, to learn . . . and to follow.

A Parent Tip

Of course we know that God watches over us, but we must also make certain that our children know that we know. And, we must behave in ways that let our children know that we know that He knows. Whew!

HONOR GOD ON THE SABBATH

Remember the Sabbath day, to keep it holy.

EXODUS 20:8 NKJV

When God gave Moses the Ten Commandments, it became perfectly clear that our Heavenly Father intends for us to make the Sabbath a holy day, a day for worship, for contemplation, for fellowship, and for rest. Yet we live in a seven-day-a-week world, a world that all too often treats Sunday as a regular workday.

How does your family observe the Lord's day? When church is over, do you treat Sunday like any other day of the week? If so, it's time to think long and hard about your family's schedule and your family's priorities.

Whenever we ignore God's commandments, we pay a price. So if you've been treating Sunday as just another day, it's time to break that habit. When Sunday rolls around, don't try to fill every spare moment. Take time to rest . . . Father's orders!

A Parent Tip

As a parent, you decide how your family will spend Sundays. Decide wisely.

Day 190

HEALTHY CHOICES

I shall yet praise him, who is the health of my countenance, and my God.

PSALM 42:11 KJV

The journey toward improved health is not only a common-sense exercise in personal discipline, it is also a spiritual journey ordained by our Creator. God does not intend that we abuse our bodies by giving in to excessive appetites or to slothful behavior. To the contrary, God has instructed us to protect our physical bodies to the greatest extent we can.

God's plan for you includes provisions for your spiritual, physical, and emotional health. But, He expects you to do your fair share of the work! In a world that is chock-full of tasty temptations, you may find it all too easy to make unhealthy choices. Your challenge, of course, is to resist those unhealthy temptations by every means you can, including prayer. And rest assured: when you ask for God's help, He will give it.

A Parent Tip

Many of the messages that stream from the media are specifically designed to sell your child products that interfere with his or her spiritual, physical, or emotional health. Help your child become a thoughtful consumer of the media's messages and the products that those messages are intended to sell.

THE SELF-FULFILLING PROPHECY

May He grant you according to your heart's desire, and fulfill all your purpose.

PSALM 20:4 NKJV

The self-fulfilling prophecy is alive, well, and living at your house. If you trust God and have faith for the future, your optimistic beliefs will give you direction and motivation. That's one reason that you should never lose hope, but certainly not the only reason. The primary reason that you, as a believer, should never lose hope, is because of God's unfailing promises.

Make no mistake about it: thoughts are powerful things: your thoughts have the power to lift you up or to hold you down. When you acquire the habit of hopeful thinking, you will have acquired a powerful tool for improving your life. So if you fall into the habit of negative thinking, think again. After all, God's Word teaches us that Christ can overcome every difficulty (John 16:33). And when God makes a promise, He keeps it.

A Talking Point

Today, talk to your daughter about the self-fulfilling prophecy.

Day 192

THE VOICE OF GOD

Listen in silence before me....

ISAIAH 41:1 NLT

Sometimes God speaks loudly and clearly. More often, He speaks in a quiet voice—and if you are wise, you will be listening carefully when He does. To do so, you must carve out quiet moments each day to study His Word and sense His direction.

Can you quiet yourself long enough to listen to your conscience? Are you attuned to the subtle guidance of your intuition? Are you willing to pray sincerely and then to wait quietly for God's response. Hopefully so. Usually God refrains from sending His messages on stone tablets or city billboards. More often, He communicates in subtler ways. If you sincerely desire to hear His voice, you must listen carefully, and you must do so in the silent corners of your quiet, willing heart.

A Quote to Talk About

When we come to Jesus stripped of pretensions, with a needy spirit, ready to listen, He meets us at the point of need.

CATHERINE MARSHALL

YOUR SPIRITUAL JOURNEY

I pray that you, being rooted and firmly established in love, may be able to comprehend with all the saints what is the breadth and width, height and depth, and to know the Messiah's love that surpasses knowledge, so you may be filled with all the fullness of God.

EPHESIANS 3:17-19 HCSB

The journey toward spiritual maturity lasts a lifetime. As Christians, we can and should continue to grow in the love and the knowledge of our Savior as long as we live. When we cease to grow, either emotionally or spiritually, we do ourselves a profound disservice. But, if we study God's Word, if we obey His commandments, and if we live in the center of His will, we will not be "stagnant" believers; we will, instead, be healthy, growing Christians.

Life is a series of decisions. Each day, we make countless decisions that can bring us closer to God . . . or not. When we live according to the principles contained in God's Holy Word, we embark upon a journey of spiritual maturity that results in life abundant and life eternal.

A Parent Tip

Thoughtful Christian parents don't follow the crowd . . . thoughtful Christian parents follow Jesus.

Day 194

FAITHFUL STEWARDSHIP

God has given gifts to each of you from his great variety of spiritual gifts. Manage them well so that God's generosity can flow through you.

1 PETER 4:10 NLT

We are challenged to be faithful stewards of the resources and talents that God has given us. But we live in a world that encourages us to do otherwise. Ours is a society that is filled to the brim with countless opportunities to squander our time, our talents, our energy, and our money. But we must beware: God warns us not to waste the blessings that He has bestowed upon us, and we must heed that warning.

Every member of your family possesses special gifts, unique talents and opportunities that can be used or not. You should value the talents that God has given you, you should nourish those talents, and you should share them with the world.

For dedicated Christian families like yours, stewardship is not something to be taken lightly. After all, God has given you countless blessings. That's why you must manage your family's resources as if they were vitally important to God, which, by the way, they are.

A Talking Point

Today, talk to your daughter about the joys and responsibilities of Christian stewardship.

THE VOICE INSIDE YOUR HEAD

I always try to do what I believe is right before God and people.

ACTS 24:16 NCV

Your conscience is an early-warning system designed to keep you out of trouble. If you listen to that voice, you'll be okay; if you ignore it, you're asking for headaches, or heartbreaks, or both.

Whenever you're about to make an important decision, you should listen carefully to the quiet voice inside. Sometimes, of course, it's tempting to do otherwise. From time to time, you'll be tempted to abandon your better judgement by ignoring your conscience. But remember: a conscience is a terrible thing to waste. So instead of ignoring that quiet little voice, pay careful attention to it. If you do, your conscience will lead you in the right direction—in fact, it's trying to lead you right now. So listen . . . and learn.

A Talking Point

Today, remind your daughter that the quiet voice inside her head will guide her down the right path if she listens carefully.

Day 196

COURTESY MATTERS

Out of respect for Christ, be courteously reverent to one another.

EPHESIANS 5:21 MSG

Did Christ instruct us in matters of etiquette and courtesy? Of course He did. Christ's instructions are clear: "In everything, therefore, treat people the same way you want them to treat you, for this is the Law and the Prophets" (Matthew 7:12 NASB). Jesus did not say, "In some things, treat people as you wish to be treated." And, He did not say, "From time to time, treat others with kindness." Christ said that we should treat others as we wish to be treated in every aspect of our daily lives. This, of course, is a tall order indeed, but as Christians, we are commanded to do our best.

Today, be a little kinder than necessary to family members, friends, and total strangers. And, as you consider all the things that Christ has done in your life, honor Him with your words and with your deeds. He expects no less, and He deserves no less.

A Parent Tip

When in doubt, do something good for somebody. That's how you'll teach your child the art and the joys of compassionate Christianity.

BEYOND THE DIFFICULTIES

When you are in distress and all these things have happened to you, you will return to the Lord your God in later days and obey Him. He will not leave you, destroy you, or forget the covenant with your fathers that He swore to them by oath, because the Lord your God is a compassionate God.

DEUTERONOMY 4:30-31 HCSB

Sometimes the traffic jams, and sometimes the dog gobbles the homework. But, when we find ourselves overtaken by the minor frustrations of life, we must catch ourselves, take a deep breath, and lift our thoughts upward. Although we are here on earth struggling to rise above the distractions of the day, we need never struggle alone. God is here—eternally and faithfully, with infinite patience and love—and, if we reach out to Him, He will restore perspective and peace to our souls.

If you find yourself enduring difficult circumstances, remember that God remains in His heaven. If you become discouraged with the direction of your day or your life, lift your thoughts and prayers to Him. He will guide you through your difficulties and beyond them.

A Quote to Talk About

When life is difficult, God wants us to have a faith that trusts and waits.

KAY ARTHUR

BIG DREAMS

With God's power working in us, God can do much, much more than anything we can ask or imagine.

EPHESIANS 3:20 NCV

Are you willing to entertain the possibility that God has big plans in store for you? Hopefully so. Yet sometimes, especially if you've recently experienced a life-altering disappointment, you may find it difficult to envision a brighter future for yourself and your family. If so, it's time to reconsider your own capabilities . . . and God's.

Your Heavenly Father created you with unique gifts and untapped talents; your job is to tap them. When you do, you'll begin to feel an increasing sense of confidence in yourself and in your future. So even if you're experiencing difficult days, don't abandon your dreams. Instead, trust that God is preparing you for greater things.

A Quote to Talk About

Sometimes our dreams were so big that it took two people to dream them.

MARIE T. FREEMAN

ENTHUSIASM FOR CHRIST

So roll up your sleeves, put your mind in gear, be totally ready to receive the gift that's coming when Jesus arrives. Don't lazily slip back into those old grooves of evil, doing just what you feel like doing. You didn't know any better then; you do now. As obedient children, let yourselves be pulled into a way of life shaped by God's life, a life energetic and blazing with holiness.

1 PETER 1:13-15 MSG

John Wesley advised, "Catch on fire with enthusiasm and people will come for miles to watch you burn." His words still ring true. When we fan the flames of enthusiasm for Christ, our faith serves as a beacon to others.

Our world desperately needs faithful parents (like you) who share the Good News of Jesus with joyful exuberance. The world desperately needs your enthusiasm and so do your children.

A Talking Point

Today, talk to your daughter about what it means to be an enthusiastic Christian.

Day 200

PRAY WITHOUT CEASING

Be cheerful no matter what; pray all the time; thank God no matter what happens. This is the way God wants you who belong to Christ Jesus to live.

1 THESSALONIANS 5:16-18 MSG

On his second missionary journey, Paul started a small church in Thessalonica. A short time later, he penned a letter that was intended to encourage the new believers at that church. Today, almost 2,000 years later, 1 Thessalonians remains a powerful, practical guide for Christian living.

In his letter, Paul advised members of the new church to "pray without ceasing." His advice applies to Christians of every generation. When we consult God on an hourly basis, we avail ourselves of His wisdom, His strength, and His love. As Corrie ten Boom observed, "Any concern that is too small to be turned into a prayer is too small to be made into a burden."

Today, make yourself a prayerful parent. Instead of turning things over in your mind, turn them over to God in prayer. Instead of worrying about your next decision, ask God to lead the way. Don't limit your prayers to meals or bedtime. Be a prayerful parent.

A Parent Tip

Absolutely no parental duty is more important than praying for your child.

QUALITY TIME, QUANTITY TIME

Teach us to number our days carefully so that we may develop wisdom in our hearts.

PSALM 90:12 HCSB

Make no mistake: caring for your family requires time—lots of time. You've probably heard about "quality time" and "quantity time." Your family needs both. So, as a responsible Christian, you should willingly invest large quantities of your time and energy in the care and nurturing of your clan.

While caring for your family, you should do your best to ensure that God remains squarely at the center of your household. When you do, God will bless you and yours in ways that you could have scarcely imagined.

A Parent Tip

The real currency of family life is time, not dollars. Wise parents give generous amounts of time to their youngsters.

Day 202

YOUR BODY, GOD'S TEMPLE

Don't you realize that all of you together are the temple of God and that the Spirit of God lives in you?

1 CORINTHIANS 3:16 NLT

Are you and your family members shaping up or spreading out? Do you and your loved ones eat sensibly and exercise regularly, or do you spend most of your time on the couch with a snack in one hand and a clicker in the other? Are you choosing to treat your bodies like temples or a trash heaps? How you answer these questions will help determine how long you live and how well you live.

Physical fitness is a choice, a choice that requires discipline—it's as simple as that. So, set a good example: Make up your mind to treat your body like a one-of-a-kind gift from God . . . because that's precisely what your body is.

A Parent Tip

Teach by example. If you make healthy habits an important part of your own lifestyle, your children will, in all likelihood, follow your example.

A LIFE OF INTEGRITY

The one who lives with integrity is righteous; his children who come after him will be happy.

PROVERBS 20:7 HCSB

Wise parents understand that integrity is a crucial building block in the foundation of a well-lived life. Integrity is built slowly over a lifetime. It is the sum of every right decision, every honest word, every noble thought, and every heartfelt prayer. It is forged on the anvil of honorable work and polished by the twin virtues of generosity and humility. Integrity is a precious thing—difficult to build, but easy to tear down; godly parents value it and protect it at all costs.

As believers in Christ, we must seek to live each day with discipline, honesty, and faith. When we do, at least two things happen: integrity becomes a habit, and God blesses us because of our obedience to Him.

A Parent Tip

What the world needs is more parents who are willing to be positive role models to their children. God wants you to be that kind of parent . . . now!

Day 204

GOD'S LESSONS

Take good counsel and accept correction—that's the way to live wisely and well.

PROVERBS 19:20 MSG

When it comes to learning life's lessons, we can either do things the easy way or the hard way. The easy way can be summed up as follows: when God teaches us a lesson, we learn it . . . the first time! Unfortunately, too many of us learn much more slowly than that.

When we resist God's instruction, He continues to teach, whether we like it or not. Our challenge, then, is to discern God's lessons from the experiences of everyday life. Hopefully, we learn those lessons sooner rather than later because the sooner we do, the sooner He can move on to the next lesson and the next, and the next.

A Parent Tip

Make continuing education an important part of your own life; your children will, in all likelihood, follow your example.

THE WISDOM OF MODERATION

Moderation is better than muscle, self-control better than political power.

PROVERBS 16:32 MSG

Moderation and wisdom are traveling companions. If we are wise, we must learn to temper our appetites, our desires, and our impulses. When we do, we are blessed, in part, because God has created a world in which temperance is rewarded and intemperance is inevitably punished.

Would you like to improve your life? Then harness your appetites and restrain your impulses. Moderation is difficult, of course; it is especially difficult in a prosperous society such as ours. But the rewards of moderation are numerous and long-lasting. Claim those rewards today. No one can force you to moderate your appetites. The decision to live temperately (and wisely) is yours and yours alone. And so are the consequences.

A Parent Tip

If you expect your daughter to have self-control, then you must have it, too. When it comes to parenting, you can't really teach it if you won't really live it.

Day 206

OPTIMISM 101

Whatever I have, wherever I am, I can make it through anything in the One who makes me who I am.

PHILIPPIANS 4:13 MSG

To be a pessimistic Christian is a contradiction in terms, yet sometimes even the most devout Christians fall prey to fear, doubt, and discouragement. But, God has a different plan for our lives. The comforting words of the 23rd Psalm remind us of God's blessings. In response to His grace, we should strive to focus our thoughts on things that are pleasing to Him, not upon things that are evil, discouraging, or frustrating.

So, the next time you find yourself mired in the pit of pessimism, remember God's Word and redirect your thoughts. This world is God's creation; look for the best in it, and trust Him to take care of the rest.

A Quote to Talk About

If you can't tell whether your glass is half-empty or half-full, you don't need another glass; what you need is better eyesight . . . and a more thankful heart.

MARIE T. FREEMAN

HIS CALLING

And don't be wishing you were someplace else or with someone else. Where you are right now is God's place for you. Live and obey and love and believe right there.

1 CORINTHIANS 7:17 MSG

It is terribly important that you heed God's calling by discovering and developing your talents and your spiritual gifts. If you seek to make a difference—and if you seek to bear eternal fruit—you must discover your gifts and begin using them for the glory of God.

Every believer has at least one gift. In John 15:16, Jesus says, "You did not choose Me, but I chose you and appointed you that you should go and bear fruit, and that your fruit should remain, that whatever you ask the Father in My name He may give you." Have you found your special calling? If not, keep searching and keep praying until you find it. God has important work for you to do, and the time to begin that work is now.

A Quote to Talk About

God has given you special talents—now it's your turn to give them back to God.

MARIE T. FREEMAN

Day 208

NOW, NOT LATER

We can't afford to waste a minute, must not squander these precious daylight hours in frivolity and indulgence . . . . Don't loiter and linger, waiting until the very last minute. Dress yourselves in Christ, and be up and about!

ROMANS 13:13-14 MSG

Are you serious about teaching your kids the wisdom of getting things done sooner rather than later? And are you willing to teach the gospel of "getting things done" by your example as well as your words? If so, your children will be the better for it.

Procrastination is, at its core, a struggle against oneself; the only antidote is action. Once we acquire the habit of doing what needs to be done when it needs to be done, we avoid untold trouble, worry, and stress. We learn to defeat procrastination by paying less attention to our fears and more attention to our responsibilities.

Life punishes procrastinators, and it does so sooner rather than later. In other words, Mom and Dad, life doesn't procrastinate. And neither should we.

A Parent Tip

As a parent, you know that procrastination is an easy habit to acquire and a difficult habit to break. When the time is right, help your child learn the value of self-discipline and the importance of doing first things first.

THE POWER OF WORDS

The wise don't tell everything they know, but the foolish talk too much and are ruined.

PROVERBS 10:14 NCV

All too often, in the rush to have ourselves heard, we speak first and think next . . . with unfortunate results. God's Word reminds us that, "Reckless words pierce like a sword, but the tongue of the wise brings healing" (Proverbs 12:18 NIV). If we seek to be a source of encouragement to friends and family, then we must measure our words carefully. Words are important: they can hurt or heal. Words can uplift us or discourage us, and reckless words, spoken in haste, cannot be erased.

Today, measure your words carefully. Use words of kindness and praise, not words of anger or derision. Remember that you have the power to heal others or to injure them, to lift others up or to hold them back. When you lift them up, your wisdom will bring healing and comfort to a world that needs both.

A Parent Tip

If you need help communicating with your child, ask God to help you find the right words to say. When you ask Him, sincerely and often, He will answer your prayers.

Day 210

AN INTENSELY BRIGHT FUTURE: YOURS

I came that they may have life, and have it abundantly.

JOHN 10:10 NASB

Are you excited about the opportunities of today and thrilled by the possibilities of tomorrow? Do you confidently expect God to lead you to a place of abundance, peace, and joy? And, when your days on earth are over, do you expect to receive the priceless gift of eternal life? If you trust God's promises, and if you have welcomed God's Son into your heart, then you believe that your future is intensely and eternally bright.

It takes courage to dream big dreams. You will discover that courage when you do three things: accept the past, trust God to handle the future, and make the most of the time He has given you today. No dreams are too big for God—not even yours. So start living—and dreaming—accordingly.

A Quote to Talk About

Allow your dreams a place in your prayers and plans. God-given dreams can help you move into the future He is preparing for you.

BARBARA JOHNSON

WHAT KIND OF EXAMPLE?

Set an example of good works yourself, with integrity and dignity in your teaching.

TITUS 2:7 HCSB

Whether we like it or not, we are role models. Hopefully, the lives we lead and the choices we make will serve as enduring examples of the spiritual abundance that is available to all who worship God and obey His commandments.

Ask yourself this question: Are you the kind of role model that you would want to emulate? If so, congratulations. But if certain aspects of your behavior could stand improvement, the best day to begin your self-improvement regimen is this one. Because whether you realize it or not, people you love are watching your behavior, and they're learning how to live. You owe it to them—and to yourself—to live righteously and well.

A Parent Tip

Give your children the gift of a lifetime. How? By being a worthy example—practice what you preach.

Day 212

TEMPORARY SETBACKS

A time to weep, and a time to laugh; a time to mourn, and a time to dance….

ECCLESIASTES 3:4 KJV

The occasional disappointments and failures of life are inevitable. Such setbacks are simply the price that we must occasionally pay for our willingness to take risks as we pursue our goals. But even when we encounter bitter disappointments, we must never lose faith.

As parents, we are far from perfect. And, without question, our children are imperfect as well. When we make mistakes, we must correct them and learn from them. And, when our children make mistakes, we must help them do likewise.

Have you or your child ever made a small mistake, a medium-sized blunder, or a big-time failure? If so, remember that God's love is permanent, but for hardworking folks (like you) failure never is.

A Talking Point

Today, remind your daughter that occasional setbacks are simply the price she must sometimes pay for trying to achieve worthwhile goals.

FINANCIAL SECURITY

Honor the Lord with your wealth and the firstfruits from all your crops. Then your barns will be full, and your wine barrels will overflow with new wine.

PROVERBS 3:9-10 NCV

The quest for financial security is a journey that leads us across many peaks and through a few unexpected valleys. When we reach the mountaintops, we find it easy to praise God and to give thanks. But, when we face disappointment or financial hardship, it seems so much more difficult to trust God's perfect plan. But, trust Him we must.

As you strive to achieve financial security for your family, remember this: The next time you find your courage tested to the limit (and it will be), lean upon God's promises. Trust His Son. Remember that God is always near and that He is your protector and your deliverer. Always.

A Quote to Talk About

If the Living Logos of God has the power to create and sustain the universe . . . . He is more than able to sustain your marriage and your ministry, your faith and your finances, your hope and your health.

ANNE GRAHAM LOTZ

Day 214

NOW IS THE TIME

So, my son, throw yourself into this work for Christ.

2 TIMOTHY 1:1 MSG

God's love for your family is deeper and more profound than you can imagine. God's love for you is so great that He sent His only Son to this earth to die for your sins and to offer you the priceless gift of eternal life. Now, you must decide whether or not to accept God's gift. Will you ignore it or embrace it? Will you return it or neglect it? Will you accept Christ's love and build a lifelong relationship with Him, or will you turn away from Him and take a different path?

Your decision to allow Christ to reign over your heart is the pivotal decision of your life. It is a decision that you cannot ignore. It is a decision that is yours and yours alone. Accept God's gift now: allow His Son to preside over your heart, your thoughts, and your life, starting this very instant.

A Parent Tip

Do you want your family members to follow in the footsteps of Jesus? Then you must lead the way. Actions speak louder than sermons . . . much louder.

FORGIVING AND FORGETTING

Real wisdom, God's wisdom, begins with a holy life and is characterized by getting along with others. It is gentle and reasonable, overflowing with mercy and blessings, not hot one day and cold the next, not two-faced.

JAMES 3:17 MSG

Do you have a tough time forgiving and forgetting? If so, welcome to the club. Most of us find it difficult to forgive the people who have hurt us. And that's too bad because life would be much simpler if we could forgive people "once and for all" and be done with it. Yet forgiveness is seldom that easy. Usually, the decision to forgive is straightforward, but the process of forgiving is more difficult. Forgiveness is a journey that requires time, perseverance, and prayer.

If you sincerely wish to forgive someone, pray for that person. And then pray for yourself by asking God to heal your heart. Don't expect forgiveness to be easy or quick, but rest assured: with God as your partner, you can forgive . . . and you will.

A Parent Tip

It starts at home, and as the parent, you're in charge of demonstrating the fine art of forgiveness. It's a big job, so don't be afraid to ask for help . . . especially God's help.

Day 216

A HELPING HAND

The greatest among you will be your servant. Whoever exalts himself will be humbled, and whoever humbles himself will be exalted.

MATTHEW 23:11-12 HCSB

Jesus has much to teach us about generosity. He teaches that the most esteemed men and women are not the self-congratulatory leaders of society but are, instead, the humblest of servants. If you were being graded on generosity, how would you score? Would you earn "A"s in philanthropy and humility? Hopefully so. But if your grades could stand a little improvement, this is the perfect day to begin.

Today, you may feel the urge to hoard your blessings. Don't do it. Instead, give generously to your neighbors, and do so without fanfare. Find a need and fill it . . . humbly. Lend a helping hand and share a word of kindness . . . anonymously. This is God's way.

A Parent Tip

Generosity is contagious; kids can catch it from their parents.

WITH GOD'S STRENGTH

Come to Me, all you who are weary and burdened, and I will give you rest. Take My yoke upon you and learn from Me, because I am gentle and humble in heart, and you will find rest for your souls. For My yoke is easy and My burden is light.

MATTHEW 11:28–30 HCSB

Are you tired? Ask God for strength. Are you frustrated or fearful? Pray as if everything depended upon God, and work as if everything depended upon you. With God's help, you will find the strength to be the kind of parent who makes your Heavenly Father beam with pride.

Perhaps you are in a hurry for God to reveal His plans for your life. If so, be forewarned: God operates on His own timetable, not yours. Sometimes, God may answer your prayers with silence, and when He does, you must patiently persevere. In times of trouble, you must remain steadfast and trust in the merciful goodness of your Heavenly Father. Whatever your problem, He can handle it. Your job is to keep persevering until He does.

A Quote to Talk About

Measure the size of the obstacles against the size of God.

BETH MOORE

Day 218

YOUR WAY OR GOD'S WAY

A man's heart plans his way, but the Lord directs his steps.

PROVERBS 16:9 NKJV

The popular song "My Way" is a perfectly good tune, but it's not a perfect guide for life. If you're looking for life's perfect prescription, you'd better forget about doing things your way and start doing things God's way. The most important decision of your life is, of course, your commitment to accept Jesus Christ as your personal Lord and Savior. And once your eternal destiny is secured, you will undoubtedly ask yourself the question "What now, Lord?" If you earnestly seek God's will for your life, you will find it...in time.

Sometimes, God's plans are crystal clear; sometimes they are not. So be patient, keep searching, and keep praying. If you do, then in time, God will answer your prayers and make His plans known. You'll discover those plans by doing things His way . . . and you'll be eternally grateful that you did.

A Quote to Talk About

Ours is an intentional God, brimming over with motive and mission. He never does things capriciously or decides with the flip of a coin.

JONI EARECKSON TADA

TRUSTING HIM COMPLETELY

I will be your God throughout your lifetime—until your hair is white with age. I made you, and I will care for you. I will carry you along and save you.

ISAIAH 46:4 NLT

God has promised to lift you up and guide your steps if you let Him do so. God has promised that when you and your family entrust your lives to Him completely and without reservation, He will give you the strength to meet any challenge, the courage to face any trial, and the wisdom to live in His righteousness.

God's hand uplifts those who turn their hearts and prayers to Him. Will you count yourself among that number? Will you accept God's peace and wear God's armor against the temptations and distractions of our dangerous world? If you do, you can live courageously and optimistically, knowing that you have been forever touched by the loving, unfailing, uplifting hand of God.

A Quote to Talk About

Snuggle in God's arms. When you are hurting, when you feel lonely or left out, let Him cradle you, comfort you, reassure you of His all-sufficient power and love.

KAY ARTHUR

Day 220

A FEARLESS WOMAN

Teach me Your way, O Lord; I will walk in Your truth.

PSALM 86:11 NKJV

The Book of Judges (chapters 4 and 5) tells the story of Deborah, the fearless woman who helped lead the army of Israel to victory over the Canaanites. Deborah was a judge and a prophetess, a woman called by God to lead her people. And when she answered God's call, she was rewarded with one of the great victories of Old Testament times. Like Deborah, all of us are called to serve our Creator. And, like Deborah, we may sometimes find ourselves facing trials that can bring trembling to the very depths of our souls. As believers, we must seek God's will and follow it.

As this day unfolds, seek God's will for your own life and obey His Word. He will give you the strength to meet any challenge, the courage to face any trial, and the wisdom to live in His righteousness and in His peace.

A Quote to Talk About

We get into trouble when we think we know what to do and we stop asking God if we're doing it.

STORMIE OMARTIAN

DISCOVERING HOPE

These things I have spoken to you, that in Me you may have peace. In the world you will have tribulation; but be of good cheer, I have overcome the world.

JOHN 16:33 NKJV

There are few sadder sights on earth than the sight of a person who has lost all hope. In difficult times, hope can be elusive, but Christians need never lose it. After all, God is good; His love endures; He has promised His children the gift of eternal life.

If you find yourself falling into the spiritual traps of worry and discouragement, consider the words of Jesus. It was Christ who promised, "In the world you will have tribulation; but be of good cheer, I have overcome the world." This world is indeed a place of trials and tribulations, but as believers, we are secure. God has promised us peace, joy, and eternal life. And, of course, God always keeps His promises.

A Parent Tip

If you want to teach your daughter how to be a hopeful Christian . . . be one.

Day 222

WHEN ANGER IS APPROPRIATE

The face of the Lord is against those who do evil.

PSALM 34:16 NKJV

Sometimes, anger can be a good thing. In the 22nd chapter of Matthew, we see how Christ responded when He confronted the evildoings of those who invaded His Father's house of worship: "And Jesus entered the temple and drove out all those who were buying and selling in the temple, and overturned the tables of the moneychangers and the seats of those who were selling doves" (v. 12 NASB). Thus, Jesus proved that righteous indignation is an appropriate response to evil.

When you come face-to-face with the devil's handiwork, don't be satisfied to remain safely on the sidelines. Instead, follow in the footsteps of your Savior. Jesus never compromised with evil, and neither should you.

A Talking Point

Today, remind your daughter that evil exists, that temptations are everywhere, and that God offers the ultimate protection.

ASKING AND RECEIVING

Ask, and it will be given to you; seek, and you will find; knock, and it will be opened to you. For everyone who asks receives, and he who seeks finds, and to him who knocks it will be opened.

MATTHEW 7:7-8 NKJV

Are you a parent who asks God for guidance and strength? If so, then you're continually inviting your Creator to reveal Himself in a variety of ways. As a follower of Christ, you must do no less.

Jesus made it clear to His disciples: they should petition God to meet their needs. So should we. Genuine, heartfelt prayer produces powerful changes in us and in our world. When we lift our hearts to God, we open ourselves to a never-ending source of divine wisdom and infinite love.

Do you have questions about your future that you simply can't answer? Do you sincerely seek to know God's purpose for your life? If so, ask Him for direction, for protection, and for strength—and then keep asking Him every day that you live. Whatever your need, no matter how great or small, pray about it and never lose hope.

A Parent Tip

If you need help, ask. And remember this: God is listening, and He wants to help you right now.

Day 224

RIGHTEOUSNESS NOW!

By this we know that we have come to know Him, if we keep His commandments.

1 JOHN 2:3 NASB

When we seek righteousness in our own lives—and when we seek the companionship of those who do likewise—we reap the spiritual rewards that God intends for us to enjoy. When we behave ourselves as godly parents, we honor God. When we live righteously and according to God's commandments, He blesses us in ways that we cannot fully understand.

Today, as you fulfill your parental responsibilities, hold fast to that which is good, and associate yourself with believers who behave themselves in like fashion. When you do, your good works will serve as a powerful example for others and as a worthy offering to your Creator.

A Talking Point

Today, talk to your daughter about the rewards of living righteously.

ACKNOWLEDGING YOUR BLESSINGS

The Lord bless you and keep you; the Lord make His face shine upon you, and be gracious to you.

NUMBERS 6:24-25 NKJV

When the demands of life leave us rushing from place to place with scarcely a moment to spare, we may fail to pause and thank our Creator for His gifts. But, whenever we neglect to give proper thanks to the Father, we suffer because of our misplaced priorities.

Today, begin making a list of your blessings. You most certainly will not be able to make a complete list, but take a few moments and jot down as many blessings as you can. Then, give thanks to the Giver of all good things: God. His love for you is eternal, as are His gifts. And it's never too soon—or too late—to offer Him thanks.

A Talking Point

Today, talk to your daughter about the need to count her blessings early and often.

Day 226

CHEERFUL CHRISTIANITY

Be cheerful. Keep things in good repair. Keep your spirits up. Think in harmony. Be agreeable. Do all that, and the God of love and peace will be with you for sure.

2 CORINTHIANS 13:11 MSG

Mrs. Charles E. Cowman, the author of the classic devotional text, *Streams in the Desert*, wrote, "Two wings are necessary to lift our souls toward God: prayer and praise. Prayer asks. Praise accepts the answer." That's why we should find the time to lift our concerns to God in prayer, and to praise Him for all that He has done. John Wesley correctly observed, "Sour godliness is the devil's religion." His words remind us that pessimism and doubt are some of the most important tools that Satan uses to achieve his objectives. Our challenge, of course, is to ensure that Satan cannot use these tools on us.

Are you a cheerful Christian? You should be! And what is the best way to attain the joy that is rightfully yours? By giving Christ what is rightfully His: your heart, your soul, and your life.

A Talking Point

Remind your daughter that cheerfulness is its own reward—but not its only reward.

A SERIES OF CHOICES

But seek first the kingdom of God and His righteousness, and all these things will be provided for you.

MATTHEW 6:33 HCSB

Your life is a series of choices. From the instant you wake up in the morning until the moment you nod off to sleep at night, you make countless decisions—decisions about the things you do, decisions about the words you speak, and decisions about the way that you choose to direct your thoughts.

As a believer who has been transformed by the love of Jesus, you have every reason to make wise choices. But sometimes, when the daily grind threatens to grind you up and spit you out, you may make choices that are displeasing to God. When you do, you'll pay a price because you'll forfeit the happiness and the peace that might otherwise have been yours.

So, as you pause to consider the kind of Christian you are—and the kind of Christian parent you want to become—ask yourself whether you're sitting on the fence or standing in the light. The choice is yours . . . and so are the consequences.

A Talking Point

Today, remind your daughter that by making wise choices, she demonstrates her love for God.

Day 228

COMPASSIONATE SERVANTS

Finally, all of you be of one mind, having compassion for one another; love as brothers, be tenderhearted, be courteous.

1 PETER 3:8 NKJV

God's Word commands us to be compassionate, generous servants to those who need our support. As believers, we have been richly blessed by our Creator. We, in turn, are called to share our gifts, our possessions, our testimonies, and our talents.

Concentration camp survivor Corrie ten Boom correctly observed, "The measure of a life is not its duration but its donation." These words remind us that the quality of our lives is determined not by what we are able to take from others, but instead by what we are able to share with others.

The thread of compassion is woven into the very fabric of Christ's teachings. If we are to be disciples of Christ, we, too, must be zealous in caring for others. Our Savior expects no less from us. And He deserves no less.

A Parent Tip

Your children need to hear that you love them . . . from you! If you're bashful, shy, or naturally uncommunicative, get over it.

CONFIDENT CHRISTIANITY

You are my hope; O Lord GOD, You are my confidence.

PSALM 71:5 NASB

We Christians have many reasons to be confident. God is in His heaven; Christ has risen, and we are the sheep of His flock. Yet sometimes, even the most devout Christians can become discouraged. Discouragement, however, is not God's way; He is a God of possibility not negativity.

Are you a confident Christian? You should be. God's grace is eternal and His promises are unambiguous. So count your blessings, not your hardships. And live courageously. God is the Giver of all things good, and He watches over you today and forever.

A Parent Tip

Do you lack confidence in your parenting skills? If so, pay careful attention to the direction of your thoughts. And while you're at it, pay careful attention to the promises contained in God's Holy Word. Remember: the more you trust God, the more confident you will become.

Day 230

THE THREAD OF GENEROSITY

The one who has two shirts must share with someone who has none, and the one who has food must do the same.

LUKE 3:11 HCSB

The thread of generosity is woven—completely and inextricably—into the very fabric of Christ's teachings. As He sent His disciples out to heal the sick and spread God's message of salvation, Jesus offered this guiding principle: "Freely you have received, freely give" (Matthew 10:8 NIV). The principle still applies.

Lisa Whelchel spoke for Christians everywhere when she observed, "The Lord has abundantly blessed me all of my life. I'm not trying to pay Him back for all of His wonderful gifts; I just realize that He gave them to me to give away." All of us have been blessed, and all of us are called to share those blessings without reservation. So, make this pledge and keep it: Be a cheerful, generous, courageous giver. The world needs your help, and you need the spiritual rewards that will be yours when you share your possessions, your talents, and your time.

A Talking Point

Today, talk to your daughter about the importance of being a cheerful giver.

OBEY AND BE BLESSED

If you obey my commands, you will remain in my love, just as I have obeyed my Father's commands and remain in his love.

JOHN 15:10 NIV

God gave us His commandments for a reason: so that we might obey them and be blessed. Elisabeth Elliot advised, "Obedience to God is our job. The results of that obedience are God's." These words should serve to remind us that obedience is imperative. But, we live in a world that presents us with countless temptations to disobey God's laws.

When we stray from God's path, we suffer. So, whenever we are confronted with sin, we have clear instructions: we must walk—or better yet run—in the opposite direction. And we must teach our children to do the same.

A Talking Point

Today, talk to your daughter about the rewards of obedience and the dangers of sin.

Day 232

ADDITIONAL RESPONSIBILITIES

So he who had received five talents came and brought five other talents, saying, "Lord, you delivered to me five talents; look, I have gained five more talents besides them." His lord said to him, "Well done, good and faithful servant; you were faithful over a few things, I will make you ruler over many things. Enter into the joy of your lord."

MATTHEW 25:20-21 NKJV

God has promised us this: when we do our duties in small matters, He will give us additional responsibilities. Sometimes, those responsibilities come when God changes the course of our lives so that we may better serve Him. Sometimes, God rewards us by answering "no" to our prayers so that He can say "yes" to a far grander request that we, with our limited understanding, would never have thought to ask for.

If you seek to be God's servant in great matters, be faithful, be patient, and be dutiful in smaller matters. Then step back and watch as God surprises you with the spectacular creativity of His infinite wisdom and His perfect plan.

A Quote to Talk About

There is something incredibly comforting about knowing that the Creator is in control of your life.

LISA WHELCHEL

SAFE IN GOD'S HANDS

When you pass through the waters, I will be with you; and through the rivers, they shall not overflow you. When you walk through the fire, you shall not be burned, nor shall the flame scorch you. For I am the Lord your God, The Holy One of Israel, your Savior.

ISAIAH 43:2-3 NKJV

As a busy parent, you know from firsthand experience that life is not always easy. But as a recipient of God's grace, you also know that you are protected by a loving Heavenly Father.

In times of trouble, God will comfort you; in times of sorrow, He will dry your tears. When you are troubled, or weak, or sorrowful, God is neither distant nor disinterested. To the contrary, God is always present and always vitally engaged in the events of your life. Reach out to Him, and build your future on the rock that cannot be shaken . . . trust in God and rely upon His provisions. He can provide everything you really need . . . and far, far more.

A Quote to Talk About

Prayer is our pathway not only to divine protection, but also to a personal, intimate relationship with God.

SHIRLEY DOBSON

Day 234

AN ATTITUDE OF GRATITUDE

Let the peace of Christ rule in your hearts, since as members of one body you were called to peace.

COLOSSIANS 3:15 NIV

For most of us, life is busy and complicated. We have countless responsibilities, some of which begin before sunrise and many of which end long after sunset. Amid the rush and crush of the daily grind, it is easy to lose sight of God and His blessings. But, when we forget to slow down and say "Thank You" to our Maker, we rob ourselves of His presence, His peace, and His joy.

Our task, as believing Christians, is to praise God many times each day. Then, with gratitude in our hearts, we can face our daily duties with the perspective and power that only He can provide.

A Quote to Talk About

If you won't fill your heart with gratitude, the devil will fill it with something else.

MARIE T. FREEMAN

DOERS OF THE WORD

Do not merely listen to the word, and so deceive yourselves. Do what it says.

JAMES 1:22 NIV

The old saying is both familiar and true: actions speak louder than words. And as believers, we must beware: Our actions should always give credence to the changes that Christ can make in the lives of those who walk with Him.

God calls upon each of us to act in accordance with His will and with respect for His commandments. If we are to be responsible believers, we must realize that it is never enough simply to hear the instructions of God; we must also live by them. And it is never enough to wait idly by while others do God's work here on earth; we, too, must act. Doing God's work is a responsibility that each of us must bear, and when we do, our loving Heavenly Father rewards our efforts with a bountiful harvest.

A Talking Point

Today, talk to your daughter about the importance of putting God's Word into action.

Day 236

FORGIVENESS STARTS AT HOME

Let all bitterness, wrath, anger, clamor, and evil speaking be put away from you, with all malice. And be kind to one another, tenderhearted, forgiving one another, just as God in Christ forgave you.

EPHESIANS 4:31-32 NKJV

Sometimes, it's easy to become angry with the people we love most, and sometimes it's hard to forgive them. After all, we know that our family will still love us no matter how angry we become. But while it's easy to become angry at home, it's usually wrong.

The next time you're tempted to lose your temper or to remain angry at a close family member, ask God to help you find the wisdom to forgive. And while you're at it, do your best to calm down sooner rather than later because peace is always beautiful, especially when it's peace at your house.

A Parent Tip

If you can control your anger, you'll help your daughter see the wisdom in controlling hers.

FACING FEARS, LIVING BOLDLY

God doesn't want us to be shy with his gifts, but bold and loving and sensible.

2 TIMOTHY 1:7 MSG

Do you prefer to face your fears rather than run from them? If so, you will be blessed because of your willingness to live courageously.

When Paul wrote Timothy, he reminded his young protégé that the God they served was a bold God, and God's spirit empowered His children with boldness also. Like Timothy, we face times of uncertainty and fear. God's message is the same to us, today, as it was to Timothy: We can live boldly because the spirit of God resides in us.

So today, as you face the challenges of everyday living, remember that God is with you . . . and you are protected.

A Talking Point

Today, remind your daughter that if the crowd is headed in the wrong direction, she should turn herself around and head in the opposite direction.

Day 238

THE PURSUIT OF GOD'S TRUTH

But grow in the grace and knowledge of our Lord and Savior Jesus Christ. To Him be the glory both now and forever. Amen.

2 PETER 3:18 NKJV

Have you established a passionate relationship with God's Holy Word? Hopefully so. After all, the Bible is a roadmap for life here on earth and for life eternal. And, as a believer who has been touched by God's grace, you are called upon to study God's Holy Word, to trust His Word, to follow its commandments, and to share its Good News with the world.

The words of Matthew 4:4 remind us that, "Man shall not live by bread alone but by every word that proceedeth out of the mouth of God" (KJV). As believers, we must study the Bible and meditate upon its meaning for our lives. Otherwise, we deprive ourselves of a priceless gift from our Creator. God's Holy Word is, indeed, a transforming gift from the Father in heaven. That's why passionate believers must never live by bread alone . . .

A Parent Tip

Take a Bible with you wherever you go. You never know when you (or someone you love) may need a spiritual boost.

CELEBRATION WITH A SMILE

Jacob said, "For what a relief it is to see your friendly smile. It is like seeing the smile of God!"

GENESIS 33:10 NLT

Life should never be taken for granted. Each day is a priceless gift from God and should be treated as such.

Hannah Whitall Smith observed, "How changed our lives would be if we could only fly through the days on wings of surrender and trust!" How true!

Today, let us celebrate life with smiles on our faces and kind words on our lips. After all, this is God's day, and He has given us clear instructions for its use. We are commanded to rejoice and be glad. So, with no further ado, let the celebration begin.

A Talking Point

Today, talk to your daughter about the need to treat every day as a cause for celebration.

Day 240

UNBENDING TRUTH

And put on the new self, which in the likeness of God has been created in righteousness and holiness of the truth. Therefore, laying aside falsehood, speak truth, each one of you, with his neighbor, for we are members of one another.

EPHESIANS 4:24-25 NASB

We live in a world that presents us with countless temptations to wander far from God's path. These temptations have the potential to destroy us, in part, because they cause us to be dishonest with ourselves and with others. Dishonesty is a habit. Once we start bending the truth, we're likely to keep bending it. A far better strategy, of course, is to acquire the habit of being completely forthright with God, with other people, and with ourselves.

Honesty is also a habit, a habit that pays powerful dividends for those who place character above convenience. So, the next time you're tempted to bend the truth—or to break it—ask yourself this simple question: "What does God want me to do?" Then listen carefully to your conscience. When you do, your actions will be honorable, and your character will take care of itself.

A Talking Point

Today, talk to your daughter about the importance of integrity.

CALMNESS IN CHAOS

You will keep in perfect peace him whose mind is steadfast, because he trusts in you.

ISAIAH 26:3 NIV

When we accept the peace of Jesus Christ into our hearts, our lives are transformed. And then, because we possess the gift of peace, we can share that gift with fellow Christians, family members, friends, and associates. If, on the other hand, we choose to ignore the gift of peace—for whatever reason—we cannot share what we do not possess.

As every parent knows, peace can be a scarce commodity in our demanding world. How, then, can we find the peace that we so desperately desire? By turning our days and our lives over to God. Elisabeth Elliot writes, "If my life is surrendered to God, all is well. Let me not grab it back, as though it were in peril in His hand but would be safer in mine!" May we give our lives, our hopes, and our prayers to the Lord, and, by doing so, accept His will and His peace.

A Parent Tip

Peace begins at home. As the parent, you're in charge of keeping the peace and sharing it. It's a big job, so don't be afraid to ask for help . . . especially God's help.

COMFORTING OTHERS

Carry each other's burdens, and in this way you will fulfill the law of Christ.

GALATIANS 6:2 NIV

We live in a world that is, on occasion, a frightening place. Sometimes, we sustain life-altering losses that are so profound and so tragic that it seems we could never recover. But, with God's help and with the help of encouraging family members and friends, we can recover.

In times of need, God's Word is clear: as believers, we must offer comfort to those in need by sharing not only our courage but also our faith. As the revivalist Vance Havner observed, "No journey is complete that does not lead through some dark valleys. We can properly comfort others only with the comfort wherewith we ourselves have been comforted of God." Enough said.

A Parent Tip

Silence is okay: Sometimes, just being there is enough. If you're not sure what to say, don't.

CONTENTMENT THAT LASTS

Serving God does make us very rich, if we are satisfied with what we have. We brought nothing into the world, so we can take nothing out. But, if we have food and clothes, we will be satisfied with that.

1 TIMOTHY 6:6-8 NCV

The preoccupation with happiness and contentment is an ever-present theme in the modern world. We are bombarded with messages that tell us where to find peace and pleasure in a world that worships materialism and wealth. But, lasting contentment is not found in material possessions; genuine contentment is a spiritual gift from God to those who trust in Him and follow His commandments. When God dwells at the center of our lives, peace and contentment will belong to us just as surely as we belong to God.

A Parent Tip

Be contented where you are, even if it's not exactly where you want to end up. God has something wonderful in store for you and your loved ones—and remember that God's timing is perfect—so be patient, trust God, do your best, and expect the best.

ENOUGH HOURS IN THE DAY?

It is good to give thanks to the Lord, and to sing praises to Your name, O Most High; to declare Your lovingkindness in the morning, and Your faithfulness every night.

PSALM 92:1-2 NKJV

Each day has 1,440 minutes—do you value your relationship with God enough to spend a few of those minutes with Him? He deserves that much of your time and more—is He receiving it from you? Hopefully so. But if you find that you're simply "too busy" for a daily chat with your Father in heaven, it's time to take a long, hard look at your priorities and your values.

As you consider your plans for the day ahead, here's a tip: organize your life around this simple principle: "God first." When you place your Creator where He belongs—at the very center of your day and your life—the rest of your priorities will fall into place.

A Parent Tip

Daily devotionals never go out of style. Are you too busy to lead a daily devotional with your family? If so, it's time to reorder your priorities.

DOUBT AND BELIEF

Immediately the father of the child cried out and said with tears, "Lord, I believe; help my unbelief!"

MARK 9:24 NKJV

Even the most faithful Christians are overcome by occasional bouts of fear and doubt. You are no different. When you feel that your faith is being tested to its limits, seek the comfort and assurance of the One who sent His Son as a sacrifice for you.

Have you ever felt your faith in God slipping away? If so, you are not alone. Every life—including yours—is a series of successes and failures, celebrations and disappointments, joys and sorrows, hopes and doubts. But even when you feel very distant from God, God is never distant from you. When you sincerely seek His presence, He will touch your heart, calm your fears, and restore your faith in the future . . . and your faith in Him.

A Parent Tip

If you're a sermon-prone parent, try this: Give fewer lectures and ask more questions.

Day 246

CONSIDERING THE CROSS

But God forbid that I should boast except in the cross of our Lord Jesus Christ, by whom the world has been crucified to me, and I to the world.

GALATIANS 6:14 NKJV

As we consider Christ's sacrifice on the cross, we should be profoundly humbled and profoundly grateful. And today, as we come to Christ in prayer, we should do so in a spirit of quiet, heartfelt devotion to the One who gave His life so that we might have life eternal.

He was the Son of God, but He wore a crown of thorns. He was the Savior of mankind, yet He was put to death on a roughhewn cross made of wood. He offered His healing touch to an unsaved world, and yet the same hands that had healed the sick and raised the dead were pierced with nails.

Christ humbled Himself on a cross—for you. As you approach Him today in prayer, think about His love and His sacrifice. And be grateful.

A Talking Point

Today, talk to your daughter about Christ's sacrifice on the cross.

A WORTHY DISCIPLE

The LORD has already told you what is good, and this is what he requires: to do what is right, to love mercy, and to walk humbly with your God.

MICAH 6:8 NLT

When Jesus addressed His disciples, He warned that each one must, "take up his cross and follow Me." The disciples must have known exactly what the Master meant. In Jesus' day, prisoners were forced to carry their own crosses to the location where they would be put to death. Thus, Christ's message was clear: in order to follow Him, Christ's disciples must deny themselves and, instead, trust Him completely. Nothing has changed since then.

If we are to be disciples of Christ, we must trust Him and place Him at the very center of our beings. Jesus never comes "next." He is always first.

Do you seek to be a worthy disciple of Christ? Then pick up His cross today and every day that you live. When you do, He will bless you now and forever.

A Parent Tip

Jesus has invited you and your daughter to become His disciples. As a caring Christian parent, you must make sure that your child understands the importance of accepting His invitation.

Day 248

FILLED WITH THE SPIRIT

Do not be drunk with wine, which will ruin you, but be filled with the Spirit.

EPHESIANS 5:18 NCV

When you are filled with the Holy Spirit, your words and deeds will reflect a love and devotion to Christ. When you are filled with the Holy Spirit, the steps of your life's journey are guided by the Lord. When you allow God's Spirit to work in you and through you, you will be energized and transformed.

Today, allow yourself to be filled with the Spirit of God. And then stand back in amazement as God begins to work miracles in your own life and in the lives of those you love.

A Quote to Talk About

The Holy Spirit will not come to us in his fullness until we see and assent to his priority—his passion for ministry.

CATHERINE MARSHALL

THE WORLD'S BEST FRIEND

Greater love has no one than this, that he lay down his life for his friends.

JOHN 15:13 NIV

Who's the best friend this world has ever had? Jesus, of course. When you invite Him into your heart, Jesus will be your friend, too . . . your friend forever. Jesus has offered to share the gifts of everlasting life and everlasting love with the world . . . and with you. If you make mistakes, He'll still be your friend. If you behave badly, He'll still love you. If you feel sorry or sad, He will help you feel better about your world and yourself.

Jesus wants you to have a happy, meaningful life. He wants you to be generous and kind, and He wants you to follow Him. The rest, of course, is up to you. You can do it! And with a friend like Jesus, you most certainly will.

A Talking Point

Today, talk to your daughter about her very best friend: Jesus.

Day 250

TOO MANY POSSESSIONS

Do not love the world or the things in the world. If you love the world, the love of the Father is not in you.

1 JOHN 2:15 NCV

On the grand stage of a well-lived life, material possessions should play a rather small role. Of course, we all need the basic necessities of life, but once we meet those needs for ourselves and for our families, the piling up of possessions creates more problems than it solves. Our real riches, of course, are not of this world. We are never really rich until we are rich in spirit.

How much stuff is too much stuff? Well, if your desire for stuff is getting in the way of your desire to know God, then you've got too much stuff—it's as simple as that. So, if you find yourself wrapped up in the concerns of the material world, it's time to reorder your priorities. And, it's time to begin storing up riches that will endure throughout eternity—the spiritual kind.

A Talking Point

Today, talk to your daughter about the dangers of materialism.

ON A MISSION

You are a chosen people. You are a kingdom of priests, God's holy nation, his very own possession. This is so you can show others the goodness of God, for he called you out of the darkness into his wonderful light.

1 PETER 2:9 NLT

Whether you realize it or not, you are on a personal mission for God. As a Christian parent, that mission is straightforward: Honor God, accept Christ as your personal Savior, and serve God's children.

Of course, you will encounter impediments as you attempt to discover the exact nature of God's purpose for your life, but you must never lose sight of the overriding purposes that God has established for all believers. You will encounter these overriding purposes again and again as you worship your Creator and study His Word.

Every day offers countless opportunities to serve God and to worship Him. When you do so, He will bless you in miraculous ways. May you continue to seek God's will, may you trust His Word, and may you place Him where He belongs: at the very center of your life.

A Quote to Talk About

I am more and more persuaded that all that is required of us is faithful seed-sowing. The harvest is bound to follow.

ANNIE ARMSTRONG

Day 252

GOD'S GUIDANCE AND YOUR PATH

Trust in the LORD with all your heart; do not depend on your own understanding. Seek his will in all you do, and he will direct your paths.

PROVERBS 3:5-6 NLT

Proverbs 3:5-6 makes this promise: if you acknowledge God's sovereignty over every aspect of your life, He will guide your path. And, as you prayerfully consider the path that God intends for you to take, here are things you should do: You should study His Word and be ever-watchful for His signs. You should associate with fellow believers who will encourage your spiritual growth. You should listen carefully to that inner voice that speaks to you in the quiet moments of your daily devotionals. And you should be patient. Your Heavenly Father may not always reveal Himself as quickly as you would like, but rest assured that God intends to use you in wonderful, unexpected ways. Your challenge is to watch, to listen, to learn . . . and to follow.

A Parent Tip

Stress safety. The teenage years can be dangerous years. As a concerned parent, you must help your teenager understand the need to behave responsibly.

THE POWER OF PRAYER

The earnest prayer of a righteous person has great power and wonderful results.

JAMES 5:16 NLT

"The power of prayer": these words are so familiar, yet sometimes we forget what they mean. Prayer is a powerful tool for communicating with our Creator; it is an opportunity to commune with the Giver of all things good. Prayer helps us find strength for today and hope for the future. Prayer is not a thing to be taken lightly or to be used infrequently.

The quality of your spiritual life will be in direct proportion to the quality of your prayer life. Prayer changes things, and it changes you. Today, instead of turning things over in your mind, turn them over to God in prayer. Instead of worrying about your next decision, ask God to lead the way. Pray constantly about things great and small. God is listening, and He wants to hear from you now.

A Talking Point

Today, talk to your daughter about the power of prayer.

Day 254

A QUIET PLACE

Now in the morning, having risen a long while before daylight, He went out and departed to a solitary place; and there He prayed.

MARK 1:35 NKJV

In the first chapter of Mark, we read that in the darkness of the early morning hours, Jesus went to a solitary place and prayed. So, too, should we. But sometimes, finding quiet moments of solitude is difficult indeed. We live in a noisy world, a world filled with distractions, frustrations, and complications. But if we allow the distractions of a clamorous world to separate us from God's peace, we do ourselves a profound disservice. Are you one of those busy parents who rushes through the day with scarcely a single moment for quiet contemplation and prayer? If so, it's time to reorder your priorities. Nothing is more important than the time you spend with your Savior. So be still and claim the inner peace that is your spiritual birthright: the peace of Jesus Christ.

A Quote to Talk About

The more complicated life becomes, the more we need to quiet our souls before God.

ELISABETH ELLIOT

SO MANY TEMPTATIONS

But remember that the temptations that come into your life are no different from what others experience. And God is faithful. He will keep the temptation from becoming so strong that you can't stand up against it. When you are tempted, he will show you a way out so that you will not give in to it.

1 CORINTHIANS 10:13 NLT

This world is filled to the brim with temptations. Some of these temptations are small; eating a second scoop of ice cream, for example, is tempting, but not very dangerous. Other temptations, however, are not nearly so harmless. The devil is working 24/7, and he's causing pain and heartache in more ways than ever before. Thankfully, in the battle against Satan, we are never alone. God is always with us, and He gives us the power to resist temptation whenever we ask Him for the strength to do so.

A Parent Tip

When your kid makes a big-time blunder (and she will), don't be too quick to bail her out. Sometimes, experience isn't just the best teacher, it's the only teacher that your child will listen to.

Day 256

THE POWER OF OUR WORDS

Watch the way you talk. Let nothing foul or dirty come out of your mouth. Say only what helps, each word a gift.

EPHESIANS 4:29 MSG

The words that we speak have the power to do great good or great harm. If we speak words of encouragement and hope, we can lift others up. And that's exactly what God commands us to do!

Sometimes, when we feel uplifted and secure, it is easy to speak kind words. Other times, when we are discouraged or tired, we can scarcely summon the energy to uplift ourselves, much less anyone else. God intends that we speak words of kindness, wisdom, and truth, no matter our circumstances, no matter our emotions. When we do, we share a priceless gift with the world, and we give glory to the One who gave His life for us. As believers, we must do no less.

A Parent Tip

Unfortunately, your daughter is growing up in a profanity-laced world. Help her understand that she will be judged by the words she speaks, and help her choose those words with care.

FAR BEYOND ENVY

So then, rid yourselves of all evil, all lying, hypocrisy, jealousy, and evil speech. As newborn babies want milk, you should want the pure and simple teaching. By it you can grow up and be saved.

1 PETER 2:1-2 NCV

Because we are frail, imperfect human beings, we are sometimes envious of others. But God's Word warns us that envy is sin. Thus, we must guard ourselves against the natural tendency to feel resentment and jealousy when other people experience good fortune. As believers, we have absolutely no reason to be envious of any people on earth. After all, as Christians we are already recipients of the greatest gift in all creation: God's grace. We have been promised the gift of eternal life through God's only begotten Son, and we must count that gift as our most precious possession.

So here's a simple suggestion that is guaranteed to bring you happiness: fill your heart with God's love, God's promises, and God's Son . . . and when you do so, leave no room for envy, hatred, bitterness, or regret.

A Talking Point

Today, remind your daughter that envy is a sin.

Day 258

FAITH THAT WORKS

You see that a person is justified by what he does and not by faith alone.

JAMES 2:24 NIV

It is important to remember that the work required to build and sustain our faith is an ongoing process. Corrie ten Boom advised, "Be filled with the Holy Spirit; join a church where the members believe the Bible and know the Lord; seek the fellowship of other Christians; learn and be nourished by God's Word and His many promises. Conversion is not the end of your journey—it is only the beginning."

The work of nourishing your faith can and should be joyful work. The hours that you invest in Bible study, prayer, meditation, and worship should be times of enrichment and celebration. And, as you continue to build your life upon a foundation of faith, you will discover that the journey toward spiritual maturity lasts a lifetime. As a child of God, you are never fully "grown": instead, you can continue "growing up" every day of your life. And that's exactly what God wants you to do.

A Talking Point

Today, remind your daughter that the path to spiritual maturity is a journey, not a destination.

FAITH VERSUS FEAR

Don't be afraid, because I am your God. I will make you strong and will help you; I will support you with my right hand that saves you.

ISAIAH 41:10 NCV

A terrible storm rose quickly on the Sea of Galilee, and the disciples were afraid. Although they had witnessed many miracles, the disciples feared for their lives, so they turned to Jesus, and He calmed the waters and the wind.

The next time you find yourself facing a fear-provoking situation, remember that the One who calmed the wind and the waves is also your personal Savior. Then ask yourself which is stronger: your faith or your fear. The answer should be obvious. So, when the storm clouds form overhead and you find yourself being tossed on the stormy seas of life, remember this: Wherever you are, God is there, too. And, because He cares for you, you are protected.

A Parent Tip

When you look into the mirror, you're gazing at the person who is the primary role model for your child. It's a big responsibility, but you—and God—are up to it!

IN FOCUS

Look straight ahead, and fix your eyes on what lies before you. Mark out a straight path for your feet; then stick to the path and stay safe. Don't get sidetracked; keep your feet from following evil.

PROVERBS 4:25-27 NLT

What is your focus today? Are you willing to focus your thoughts and energies on God's blessings and upon His will for your life? Or will you turn your thoughts to other things? This day—and every day hereafter—is a chance to celebrate the life that God has given you. It's also a chance to give thanks to the One who has offered you more blessings than you can possibly count.

Today, why not focus your thoughts on the joy that is rightfully yours in Christ? Why not take time to celebrate God's glorious creation? Why not trust your hopes instead of your fears? When you do, you will think optimistically about yourself, your family, and your world . . . and then share your optimism with others. They'll be better for it, and so will you.

A Quote to Talk About

Jesus challenges you and me to keep our focus daily on the cross of His will if we want to be His disciples.

ANNE GRAHAM LOTZ

A TERRIFIC TOMORROW

"I say this because I know what I am planning for you," says the Lord. "I have good plans for you, not plans to hurt you. I will give you hope and a good future."

JEREMIAH 29:11 NCV

How bright do you believe your future to be? Well, if you're a faithful believer, God has plans for you that are so bright that you'd better pack several pairs of sunglasses and a lifetime supply of sunblock!

The way that you think about your future will play a powerful role in determining how things turn out (it's called the "self-fulfilling prophecy," and it applies to everybody, including you). So here's another question: Are you expecting a terrific tomorrow, or are you dreading a terrible one? The answer to that question will have a powerful impact on the way tomorrow unfolds.

Today, as you live in the present and look to the future, remember that God has an amazing plan for you. Act—and believe—accordingly. And one more thing: don't forget the sunblock.

A Quote to Talk About

Do not limit the limitless God! With Him, face the future unafraid because you are never alone.

MRS. CHARLES E. COWMAN

Day 262

THE BEST POLICY

The godly are directed by their honesty.

PROVERBS 11:5 NLT

From the time we are children, we are taught that honesty is the best policy, but sometimes, being honest is hard. So, we convince ourselves that it's alright to tell "little white lies." But there's a problem: Little white lies tend to grow up, and when they do, they cause havoc and pain in our lives.

For Christians, the issue of honesty is not a topic for debate. Honesty is not just the best policy, it is God's policy, pure and simple. And if we are to be servants worthy of our Savior, Jesus Christ, we must avoid all lies, white or otherwise. So, if you're tempted to sow the seeds of deception (perhaps in the form of a "harmless" white lie), resist that temptation. Truth is God's way, and a lie—of whatever color—is not.

A Parent Tip

In every family, truth starts at the top. So live your life—and raise your kids—accordingly.

IMPERFECT BEINGS, IMPERFECT FAITH

The one who trusts in the Lord will be happy.

PROVERBS 16:20 HCSB

Why are we humans plagued by worry? Because we are imperfect beings with imperfect faith. Even though we are Christians who have been given the assurance of salvation—even though we are Christians who have received the promise of God's love and protection—we find ourselves fretting over the countless details of everyday life. Jesus understood our concerns when He spoke the reassuring words found in Matthew 6: "Therefore I tell you, do not worry about your life . . ."

As you consider the promises of Jesus, remember that God still sits in His heaven and you are His beloved child. Then, perhaps, you will worry a little less and trust God a little more, and that's as it should be because God is trustworthy . . . and you are protected.

A Quote to Talk About

Remember always that there are two things which are more utterly incompatible even than oil and water, and these two are trust and worry.

HANNAH WHITALL SMITH

Day 264

SO LAUGH!

A happy heart makes the face cheerful....

PROVERBS 15:13 NIV

Laughter is God's gift, and He intends that we enjoy it. Yet sometimes, because of the inevitable stresses of everyday life, laughter seems only a distant memory. As Christians we have every reason to be cheerful and to be thankful. Our blessings from God are beyond measure, starting, of course, with a gift that is ours for the asking, God's gift of salvation through Christ Jesus.

Few things in life are more absurd than the sight of a grumpy Christian. So today, as you go about your daily activities, approach life with a grin and a chuckle. After all, God created laughter for a reason...to use it. So laugh!

A Parent Tip

As a parent, it's up to you to make certain that your house is a place where everybody can expect to have good clean fun and plenty of laughs. How can you do so? By making certain that the good clean fun begins with you.

SHARING THE GOOD NEWS

As you go, announce this: "The kingdom of heaven has come near."

MATTHEW 10:7 HCSB

The Good News of Jesus Christ should be shouted from the rooftops by believers the world over. But all too often, it is not. For a variety of reasons, many Christians keep their beliefs to themselves, and when they do, the world suffers because of their failure to speak up.

As believers, we are called to share the transforming message of Jesus with our families, with our neighbors, and with the world. Jesus commands us to become fishers of men. And, the time to go fishing is now. We must share the Good News of Jesus Christ today—tomorrow may indeed be too late.

A Quote to Talk About

Our commission is quite specific. We are told to be His witness to all nations. For us, as His disciples, to refuse any part of this commission frustrates the love of Jesus Christ, the Son of God.

CATHERINE MARSHALL

Day 266

WISDOM IN A DONUT SHOP

My cup runs over. Surely goodness and mercy shall follow me all the days of my life; and I will dwell in the house of the Lord Forever.

PSALM 23:5-6 NKJV

Many years ago, this rhyme was posted on the wall of a small donut shop:

As you travel through life brother,
Whatever be your goal,
Keep your eye upon the donut,
And not upon the hole.

These simple words remind us of a profound truth: we should spend more time looking at the things we have, not worrying about the things we don't have.

When you think about it, you've got more blessings than you can count. So make it a habit to thank God for the gifts He's given you, not the gifts you wish He'd given you.

A Parent Tip

Your attitude toward the future will help create your future. You might as well put the self-fulfilling prophecy to work for you and your family. Besides, life is far too short to be a pessimist.

PLEASING GOD

So we make it our goal to please him . . . .

2 CORINTHIANS 5:9 NIV

When God made you, He equipped you with an array of talents and abilities that are uniquely yours. It's up to you to discover those talents and to use them, but sometimes the world will encourage you to do otherwise. At times, society will attempt to cubbyhole you, to standardize you, and to make you fit into a particular, preformed mold. Perhaps God has other plans.

Sometimes, because you're an imperfect human being, you may become so wrapped up in meeting society's expectations that you fail to focus on God's expectations. To do so is a mistake of major proportions—don't make it. Instead, seek God's guidance as you focus your energies on becoming the best "you" that you can possibly be. And, when it comes to matters of conscience, seek approval not from your peers, but from your Creator.

A Parent Tip

You know that your child is a unique gift from God . . . make sure that your child hears that message every day . . . from you.

COMMUNITY LIFE

Regarding life together and getting along with each other, you don't need me to tell you what to do. You're God-taught in these matters. Just love one another!

1 THESSALONIANS 4:9 MSG

As we travel along life's road, we build lifelong relationships with a small, dear circle of family and friends. And how best do we build and maintain these relationships? By following the Word of God. Healthy relationships are built upon honesty, compassion, responsible behavior, trust, and optimism. Healthy relationships are built upon the Golden Rule. Healthy relationships are built upon sharing and caring. All of these principles are found time and time again in God's Holy Word. When we read God's Word and follow His commandments, we enrich our own lives and the lives of those who are closest to us.

A Parent Tip

Be a participating parent. Let your child and your child's teachers know that you're available, responsive, helpful, and involved.

WHEN THE ANSWER IS "NO"

"For my thoughts are not your thoughts, neither are your ways my ways," declares the LORD. "As the heavens are higher than the earth, so are my ways higher than your ways and my thoughts that your thoughts."

ISAIAH 55:8-9 NIV

God answers our prayers. What God does not do is this: He does not always answer our prayers as soon as we might like, and He does not always answer our prayers by saying "Yes." God isn't an order-taker, and He's not some sort of cosmic vending machine. Sometimes—even when we want something very badly—our loving Heavenly Father responds to our requests by saying "No," and we must accept His answer, even if we don't understand it.

God answers prayers not only according to our wishes but also according to His master plan. We cannot know that plan, but we can know the Planner and we must trust His wisdom, His righteousness, and His love.

A Parent Tip

Sometimes, the answer to prayer is "No." God doesn't grant all of our requests, nor should He. We must help our children understand that our prayers are answered by a sovereign, all-knowing God, and that we must trust His answers.

Day 270

ABOVE AND BEYOND OUR CIRCUMSTANCES

We take the good days from God—why not also the bad days?

JOB 2:10 MSG

All of us face difficult days. Sometimes even the most devout Christian parents can become discouraged, and you are no exception. After all, you live in a world where expectations can be high and demands can be even higher.

If you find yourself enduring difficult circumstances, remember that God remains in His heaven. If you become discouraged with the direction of your day or your life, turn your thoughts and prayers to Him. He is a God of possibility, not negativity. He will guide you through your difficulties and beyond them . . . far beyond.

A Quote to Talk About

Worry is the senseless process of cluttering up tomorrow's opportunities with leftover problems from today.

BARBARA JOHNSON

TAKING UP THE CROSS

Then He said to them all, "If anyone wants to come with Me, he must deny himself, take up his cross daily, and follow Me."

LUKE 9:23 HCSB

When we have been saved by Christ, we can, if we choose, become passive Christians. We can sit back, secure in our own salvation, and let other believers spread the healing message of Jesus. But to do so is wrong. Instead, we are commanded to become disciples of the One who has saved us. When Jesus addressed His disciples, He warned them that each one must, "take up his cross daily and follow Me" (Luke 9:23 NIV). Christ's message was clear: in order to follow Him, Christ's disciples must deny themselves and, instead, trust Him completely. Nothing has changed.

Do you seek to fulfill God's purpose for your life? Then follow Christ. Follow Him by picking up His cross today and every day that you live. Then, you will quickly discover that Christ's love has the power to change everything, including you.

A Parent Tip

As parents, we must also ask ourselves a question: Do our children know what we think about Jesus? And if not, why not?

Day 272

ENCOURAGEMENT NOW!

Bright eyes cheer the heart; good news strengthens the bones.

PROVERBS 15:30 HCSB

Barnabas, a man whose name meant "Son of Encouragement," was a leader in the early Christian church. He was known for his kindness and for his ability to encourage others. Because of Barnabas, many people were introduced to Christ. And today, as believers living in a difficult world, we must seek to imitate the "Son of Encouragement."

We imitate Barnabas when we speak kind words to our families and to our friends. We imitate Barnabas when our actions give credence to our beliefs. We imitate Barnabas when we are generous with our possessions and with our praise. We imitate Barnabas when we give hope to the hopeless and encouragement to the downtrodden.

Today, be like Barnabas: become a source of encouragement to those who cross your path. When you do so, you will quite literally change the world, one person—and one moment—at a time.

A Parent Tip

Your children will learn how to treat others by watching you; be courteous to everyone, starting with those who live under your roof.

A PASSION FOR LIFE

But those who wait upon God get fresh strength. They spread their wings and soar like eagles, they run and don't get tired, they walk and don't lag behind.

ISAIAH 40:31 MSG

Are you enthusiastic about your life and your faith? Hopefully so. But if your zest for life has waned, it is now time to redirect your efforts and recharge your spiritual batteries. And that means refocusing your priorities (by putting God first) and counting your blessings (instead of your troubles).

Nothing is more important than your wholehearted commitment to your Creator and to His only begotten Son. Your faith must never be an afterthought; it must be your ultimate priority, your ultimate possession, and your ultimate passion. When you become passionate about your faith, you'll become passionate about your life, too. And God will smile.

A Parent Tip

Your children will learn about life from many sources; the most important source should be you. But remember that the lectures you give are never as important as the ones you live.

Day 274

THE GREATEST OF THESE

But now abide faith, hope, love, these three; but the greatest of these is love.

1 CORINTHIANS 13:13 NASB

The beautiful words of 1st Corinthians 13 remind us that love is God's commandment: Faith is important, of course. So, too, is hope. But, love is more important still. We are commanded (not advised, not encouraged . . . commanded!) to love one another just as Christ loved us (John 13:34). That's a tall order, but as Christians, we are obligated to follow it.

Christ showed His love for us on the cross, and we are called upon to return Christ's love by sharing it. Today, let us spread Christ's love to our families, friends, and even strangers, so that through us, others might come to know Him.

A Parent Tip

Parental love should be demonstrated with deeds, not just announced with words. You demonstrate your love by giving of yourself and your time. While you're with your child, be sure to watch carefully and listen with your ears, your eyes, and your heart. And remember: wise parents pay careful attention to the things their children don't say.

THE CORNERSTONE

Let us fix our eyes on Jesus, the author and perfecter of our faith, who for the joy set before him endured the cross, scorning its shame, and sat down at the right hand of the throne of God.

HEBREWS 12:2 NIV

Is Christ the focus of your family and your life? Are you fired with enthusiasm for Him? Are you an energized Christian who allows God's Son to reign over every aspect of your day? Make no mistake: that's exactly what God intends for you to do.

God has given you the gift of eternal life through His Son. In response to God's priceless gift, you are instructed to focus your thoughts, your prayers, and your energies upon God and His only begotten Son. To do so, you must resist the subtle yet powerful temptation to become a "spiritual dabbler." A person who dabbles in the Christian faith is unwilling to place God above all other things. Resist that temptation; make God the cornerstone and the touchstone of your life. When you do, He will give you all the strength and wisdom you need to live victoriously for Him.

A Talking Point

Today, talk to your daughter about the need to focus on Jesus.

Day 276

IN A HURRY?

The Lord is good to those who wait for Him, to the soul who seeks Him. It is good that one should hope and wait quietly for the salvation of the Lord.

LAMENTATIONS 3:25-26 NKJV

Are you in a hurry? If so, you may be in for a few disappointments. Why? Because life has a way of unfolding according to God's timetable, not yours. That's why life requires patience . . . and lots of it!

Lamentations 3:25-26 reminds us that, "The Lord is wonderfully good to those who wait for him and seek him. So it is good to wait quietly for salvation from the Lord" (NIV). But, for most of us, waiting quietly for God is difficult because we're in such a hurry for things to happen!

The next time you find your patience tested to the limit, slow down and trust God. Sometimes, we must wait patiently for Him, and that's as it should be. After all, think how patient God has been with us.

A Parent Tip

Every family puts something or someone in first place. Does God occupy first place in your family? If so, congratulations! If not, it's time to reorder your priorities.

KEEPING POSSESSIONS IN PERSPECTIVE

And He told them, "Watch out and be on guard against all greed, because one's life is not in the abundance of his possessions."

LUKE 12:15 HCSB

All too often, we focus our thoughts and energies on the accumulation of earthly treasures, leaving precious little time to accumulate the only treasures that really matter: the spiritual kind. Our material possessions have the potential to do great good or terrible harm, depending upon how we choose to use them. As believers, our instructions are clear: we must use our possessions in accordance with God's commandments, and we must be faithful stewards of the gifts He has seen fit to bestow upon us.

Today, let us honor God by placing no other gods before Him. God comes first; everything else comes next—and "everything else" most certainly includes all of our earthly possessions.

A Talking Point

Today, remind your daughter to keep material possessions in their proper perspective.

Day 278

SPIRITUAL RENEWAL

Now we look inside, and what we see is that anyone united with the Messiah gets a fresh start, is created new. The old life is gone; a new life burgeons! Look at it!

2 CORINTHIANS 5:17 MSG

Even the most inspired Christian parents can, from time to time, find themselves running on empty. The demands of daily life can drain us of our strength and rob us of the joy that is rightfully ours in Christ.

Are you tired or troubled? Turn your heart toward God in prayer. Are you weak or worried? Take the time—or, more accurately, make the time—to delve deeply into God's Holy Word. Are you spiritually depleted? Call upon fellow believers to support you, and call upon Christ to renew your spirit and your life. When you do, you'll discover that the Creator of the universe stands always ready and always able to create a new sense of wonderment and joy in you.

A Parent Tip

Getting enough sleep? If you find yourself short on patience, perhaps you're also short on sleep. If so, turn off the TV and go to bed. As your energy returns, so will your patience.

HIS TRANSFORMING POWER

Your old sinful self has died, and your new life is kept with Christ in God.

COLOSSIANS 3:3 NCV

God's has the power to transform your day and your life. Your task is to accept Christ's grace with a humble, thankful heart as you receive the "new life" that can be yours through Him.

Righteous believers who fashion their days around Jesus see the world differently; they act differently, and they feel differently about themselves and their neighbors. Hopefully, you, too, will be such a believer.

Do you desire to improve some aspect of your life? If so, don't expect changing circumstances to miraculously transform you into the person you want to become. Transformation starts with God, and it starts in the quiet corners of a willing human heart—like yours.

A Parent Tip

Don't be too hard on yourself. You don't have to be a perfect parent to be a godly one. Do the best you can, and leave the rest up to God.

Day 280

SHARING WORDS OF HOPE

Let us think about each other and help each other to show love and do good deeds.

HEBREWS 10:24 NCV

Hope, like other human emotions, is contagious. When we associate with hope-filled Christians, we are encouraged by their faith and optimism. But, if we spend too much time in the company of naysayers and pessimists, our attitudes, like theirs, tend to be cynical and negative.

Are you a hopeful, optimistic, encouraging believer? And do you associate with like-minded people? Hopefully so. As a faithful follower of the One from Galilee, you have every reason to be hopeful, and you have every reason to share your hopes with others. So today, look for reasons to celebrate God's endless blessings. And while you're at it, look for people who will join you in the celebration. You'll be better for their company, and they'll be better for yours.

A Talking Point

Today, talk to your daughter about the rewards of being an optimistic Christian.

FOR ALL ETERNITY

"I assure you: Anyone who hears My word and believes Him who sent Me has eternal life and will not come under judgment, but has passed from death to life."

JOHN 5:24–25 HCSB

As mere mortals, our vision for the future, like our lives here on earth, is limited. God's vision is not burdened by such limitations: His plans extend throughout all eternity. Thus, God's plans for you are not limited to the ups and downs of everyday life. Your Heavenly Father has bigger things in mind . . . much bigger things.

Let us praise the Creator for His priceless gift, and let us share the Good News with all who cross our paths. We return our Father's love by accepting His grace and by sharing His message and His love. When we do, we are blessed here on earth and throughout all eternity.

A Parent Tip

God has created heaven and given you a way to get there. The rest is up to you. Make sure your children know the way.

Day 282

FAITH THAT MOVES MOUNTAINS

I assure you: If anyone says to this mountain, "Be lifted up and thrown into the sea," and does not doubt in his heart, but believes that what he says will happen, it will be done for him.

MARK 11:23 HCSB

Because we live in a demanding world, all of us have mountains to climb and mountains to move. Moving those mountains requires faith.

Are you a mountain mover whose faith is evident for all to see? Hopefully so. God needs more parents who are willing to move mountains for His glory and for His kingdom.

God walks with you, ready and willing to strengthen you. Accept His strength today. And remember—Jesus taught His disciples that if they had faith, they could move mountains. You can too . . . so with no further ado, let the mountain-moving begin.

A Talking Point

Today, remind your daughter that genuine faith, plus hard work, can move mountains.

PLANS: YOURS AND GOD'S

People may make plans in their minds, but the Lord decides what they will do.

PROVERBS 16:9 NCV

If you're like most people, you want things to happen according to your wishes and according to your timetable. But sometimes, God has other plans . . . and He always has the final word.

Are you embittered by a personal tragedy that you did not deserve and cannot understand? If so, it's time to make peace with life. It's time to forgive others, and, if necessary, to forgive yourself. It's time to accept the unchangeable past, to embrace the priceless present, and to have faith in the promise of tomorrow. It's time to trust God completely. And it's time to reclaim the peace—His peace—that can and should be yours. So, if you've encountered unfortunate circumstances that are beyond your power to control, accept those circumstances . . . and trust God. When you do, you can be comforted in the knowledge that your Creator is both loving and wise, and that He understands His plans perfectly, even when you do not.

A Talking Point

Today, talk to your daughter about the need to trust God's timetable.

THE SEARCH FOR SIGNIFICANCE

For everything, absolutely everything, above and below, visible and invisible, rank after rank after rank of angels—everything got started in him and finds its purpose in him.

COLOSSIANS 1:16 MSG

God has things He wants you to do and places He wants you to go. The most important decision of your life is your commitment to accept Jesus Christ as your personal Lord and Savior. And, once your eternal destiny is secured, you will undoubtedly ask yourself the question "What's next?" If you earnestly seek God's will for your life, you will find it...in time.

You may be certain that God is planning to use you and your family members in surprising, wonderful ways. And you may be certain that He intends to lead you along a path of His choosing. Your task is to watch for His signs, to listen to His words, to obey His commandments, and to follow where He leads.

A Quote to Talk About

Jesus was the Savior Who would deliver them not only from the bondage of sin but also from meaningless wandering through life.

ANNE GRAHAM LOTZ

THE JOYS OF FRIENDSHIP

I give thanks to my God for every remembrance of you.

PHILIPPIANS 1:3 HCSB

What is a friend? The dictionary defines the word friend as "a person who is attached to another by feelings of affection or personal regard." This definition is accurate, as far as it goes, but when we examine the deeper meaning of friendship, so many more descriptors come to mind: trustworthiness, loyalty, helpfulness, kindness, encouragement, humor, and cheerfulness, to mention but a few.

Today, as you consider the many blessings that God has given you, remember to thank Him for the friends He has chosen to place along your path. May you be a blessing to them, and may they richly bless you today, tomorrow, and every day that you live.

A Parent Tip

Teach the importance of integrity every day, and, if necessary, use words.

READY. SET. GO!

Do not neglect the gift that is in you.

1 TIMOTHY 4:14 HCSB

God has given you talents and opportunities that are uniquely yours. Are you willing to use your gifts in the way that God intends? And are you willing to summon the discipline that is required to develop your talents and to hone your skills? That's precisely what God wants you to do, and that's precisely what you should desire for yourself.

As you seek to expand your talents, you will undoubtedly encounter stumbling blocks along the way, such as the fear of rejection or the fear of failure. When you do, don't stumble! Just continue to refine your skills, and offer your services to God. And when the time is right, He will use you—but it's up to you to be thoroughly prepared when He does.

A Talking Point

Today, talk to your daughter about making the most of the opportunities God has given her.

GREAT IS THY FAITHFULNESS

God, who got you started in this spiritual adventure, shares with us the life of his Son and our Master Jesus. He will never give up on you.

1 CORINTHIANS 1:9 MSG

God is faithful to us even when we are not faithful to Him. God keeps His promises to us even when we stray far from His will. He continues to love us even when we disobey His commandments. But God does not force His blessings upon us. If we are to experience His love and His grace, we must claim them for ourselves.

Are you tired, discouraged, or fearful? Be comforted: God is with you. Are you confused? Listen to the quiet voice of your Heavenly Father. Are you bitter? Talk with God and seek His guidance. Are you celebrating a great victory? Thank God and praise Him. He is the Giver of all things good. In whatever condition you find yourself, trust God and be comforted. The Father is with you.

A Parent Tip

In every family, trust starts with the older generation and works its way down to the younger ones. We must teach our children how to be trustworthy by being trustworthy. There simply is no other way.

Day 288

INFINITE POSSIBILITIES

Is anything too hard for the LORD?

GENESIS 18:14 KJV

Ours is a God of infinite possibilities. But sometimes, because of limited faith and limited understanding, we wrongly assume that God cannot or will not intervene in the affairs of mankind. Such assumptions are simply wrong.

Are you afraid to ask God to do big things in your life? Is your faith threadbare and worn? If so, it's time to abandon your doubts and reclaim your faith in God's promises. God's Holy Word makes it clear: absolutely nothing is impossible for the Lord. And since the Bible means what it says, you can be comforted in the knowledge that the Creator of the universe can do miraculous things in your own life and in the lives of your loved ones. Your challenge, as a believer, is to take God at His word, and to expect the miraculous.

A Quote to Talk About

We will see more and more that we are chosen not because of our ability, but because of the Lord's power, which will be demonstrated in our not being able.

CORRIE TEN BOOM

GOD'S TIMETABLE

Therefore humble yourselves under the mighty hand of God, that He may exalt you at the proper time, casting all your anxiety on Him, because He cares for you.

1 PETER 5:6-7 NASB

Sometimes, the hardest thing to do is to wait. This is especially true when we're in a hurry and when we want things to happen now, if not sooner! But God's plan does not always happen in the way that we would like or at the time of our own choosing. Our task—as believing Christians who trust in a benevolent, all knowing Father—is to wait patiently for God to reveal Himself.

We human beings are, by nature, impatient. We know what we want, and we know exactly when we want it: RIGHT NOW! But, God knows better. He has created a world that unfolds according to His own timetable, not ours . . . thank goodness!

A Talking Point

Today, remind your daughter that God's timing is always best.

STANDING UP FOR OUR FAITH

Keep your eyes open, hold tight to your convictions, give it all you've got, be resolute.

1 CORINTHIANS 16:13 MSG

Are you a parent whose faith is obvious to your family and to the world, or are you a spiritual shrinking violet? God needs more parents who are willing to stand up and be counted for Him.

Genuine faith is never meant to be locked up in the heart of a believer; to the contrary, it is meant to be shared. And a man who wishes to share God's Good News with the world should begin by sharing that message with his own family.

Through every triumph and tragedy, God will stand by your side and strengthen you . . . if you have faith in Him. Jesus taught His disciples that if they had faith, they could move mountains. You can too, and so can your family . . . if you have faith.

A Parent Tip

Faith in God is contagious, and when it comes to your child's spiritual journey, no one's faith is more contagious than yours! Act, pray, praise, and trust God with the certain knowledge that your child is watching . . . carefully!

GOOD THINKING

Be careful what you think, because your thoughts run your life.

PROVERBS 4:23 NCV

Are you an upbeat believer? Do you regularly put a smile on your face? Hopefully so. After all, when you decided to allow Christ to rule over your heart, you entitled yourself to share in His promise of spiritual abundance and eternal joy. But sometimes, when pessimism and doubt invade your thoughts, you won't feel like celebrating. Why? Because thoughts are intensely powerful things.

Are you fearful, angry, bored, or worried? Are you so preoccupied with the concerns of this day that you fail to thank God for the promise of eternity? If so, spend more time thinking about your blessings, and less time fretting about your hardships. Then, take time to thank the Giver of all things good for gifts that are, in truth, far too numerous to count.

A Parent Tip

Kids are amazingly intuitive. Believe it or not, your daughter is probably a mind reader. If she's like most kids, she is surprisingly sensitive. So do yourself and your child a favor: be careful with your thoughts as well as your actions.

Day 292

THE LESSONS OF TOUGH TIMES

I waited patiently for the Lord, and He turned to me and heard my cry for help. He brought me up from a desolate pit, out of the muddy clay, and set my feet on a rock, making my steps secure. He put a new song in my mouth, a hymn of praise to our God.

PSALM 40:1-3 HCSB

Have you experienced a recent setback? If so, look for the lesson that God is trying to teach you. Instead of complaining about life's sad state of affairs, learn what needs to be learned, change what needs to be changed, and move on. View failure as an opportunity to reassess God's will for your life. View life's inevitable disappointments as opportunities to learn more about yourself and your world.

Life can be difficult at times. And everybody makes mistakes. Your job is to make them only once.

A Quote to Talk About

God is able to take mistakes, when they are committed to Him, and make of them something for our good and for His glory.

RUTH BELL GRAHAM

GOD'S FORGIVENESS

If we confess our sins to him, he is faithful and just to forgive us and to cleanse us from every wrong.

1 JOHN 1:9 NLT

The Bible promises you this: When you ask God for forgiveness, He will give it. No questions asked; no explanations required. God's power to forgive, like His love, is infinite. Despite your sins, God offers immediate forgiveness. And it's time to take Him up on His offer.

When it comes to forgiveness, God doesn't play favorites and neither should you. You should forgive all the people who have harmed you (not just the people who have asked for forgiveness or the ones who have made restitution). Complete forgiveness is God's way, and it should be your way, too. Anything less is not enough.

A Quote to Talk About

Forgiveness is actually the best revenge because it not only sets us free from the person we forgive, but it frees us to move into all that God has in store for us.

STORMIE OMARTIAN

Day 294

HIS RIGHTFUL PLACE

Do not worship any other gods besides me.

EXODUS 20:3 NLT

When Jesus was tempted by Satan, the Master's response was unambiguous. Jesus chose to worship the Lord and serve Him only. We, as followers of Christ, must follow in His footsteps by placing God first.

When we place God in a position of secondary importance, we do ourselves great harm. When we allow temptations or distractions to come between us and our Creator, we suffer. But, when we imitate Jesus and place the Lord in His rightful place—at the center of our lives—then we claim spiritual treasures that will endure forever.

A Talking Point

Today, talk to your daughter about the need to put God first in every aspect of her life.

THE SOURCE OF OUR COMFORT

When I am filled with cares, Your comfort brings me joy.

PSALM 94:19 HCSB

In times of adversity, we are wise to remember the words of Jesus, who, when He walked on the water, reassured His disciples, saying, "Take courage! It is I. Don't be afraid" (Matthew 14:27 NIV). Then, with Christ on His throne—and with trusted friends and loving family members at our sides—we can face our fears with courage and with faith.

Is someone in your family facing a difficult challenge? If so, remember that no problem is too big for God . . . not even yours.

A Parent Tip

Never confuse encouragement with pity. Pity parties are best left unattended by you and your family.

Day 296

MOVING ON

"You have heard that it was said, 'You shall love your neighbor and hate your enemy.' But I say to you, love your enemies, bless those who curse you, do good to those who hate you, and pray for those who spitefully use you and persecute you, that you may be sons of your Father in heaven."

MATTHEW 5:43-45 NKJV

Sometimes, people can be discourteous and cruel. Sometimes people can be unfair, unkind, and unappreciative. Sometimes people get angry and frustrated. So what's a Christian to do? God's answer is straightforward: forgive, forget, and move on. In Luke 6:37, Jesus instructs, "Do not judge, and you will not be judged. Do not condemn, and you will not be condemned. Forgive, and you will be forgiven" (HCSB).

Today and every day, make sure that you're quick to forgive others for their shortcomings. And when other people misbehave (as they most certainly will from time to time), don't pay too much attention. Just forgive those people as quickly as you can, and try to move on . . . as quickly as you can.

A Quote to Talk About

Some folks cause happiness wherever they go, others whenever they go.

BARBARA JOHNSON

RELYING UPON HIM

Be humble under God's powerful hand so he will lift you up when the right time comes. Give all your worries to him, because he cares about you.

1 PETER 5:6-7 NCV

God is a never-ending source of support and courage for those of us who call upon Him. When we are weary, He gives us strength. When we see no hope, God reminds us of His promises. When we grieve, God wipes away our tears.

Do the demands of this day threaten to overwhelm you? If so, you must rely not only upon your own resources but also upon the promises of your Father in heaven. God will hold your hand and walk with you every day of your life if you let Him. So even if your circumstances are difficult, trust the Father. His love is eternal and His goodness endures forever.

A Quote to Talk About

When we think we can't go one more step, when the race becomes painful beyond endurance, when our hearts feel heavy, when our minds become dull, when our spirits are burned out, we have the Parakletos [Holy Spirit], Who comes alongside us, puts His everlasting arms around us, and gently walks with us to the finish.

ANNE GRAHAM LOTZ

Day 298

GROWING IN CHRIST

When I was a child, I spoke and thought and reasoned as a child does. But when I grew up, I put away childish things.

1 CORINTHIANS 13:11 NLT

The journey toward spiritual maturity lasts a lifetime. As Christians, we can and should continue to grow in the love and the knowledge of our Savior as long as we live. Norman Vincent Peale had the following advice for believers of all ages: "Ask the God who made you to keep remaking you." That advice, of course, is perfectly sound, but often ignored.

When we cease to grow, either emotionally or spiritually, we do ourselves a profound disservice. But, if we study God's Word, if we obey His commandments, and if we live in the center of His will, we will not be "stagnant" believers; we will, instead, be growing Christians . . . and that's exactly what God wants for our lives.

A Quote to Talk About

No matter what we are going through, no matter how long the waiting for answers, of one thing we may be sure. God is faithful. He keeps His promises. What He starts, He finishes . . . including His perfect work in us.

GLORIA GAITHER

RELATIONSHIPS BUILT UPON HONESTY

The one who lives with integrity lives securely, but whoever perverts his ways will be found out.

PROVERBS 10:9 HCSB

Lasting relationships are built upon a foundation of honesty and trust. It has been said on many occasions that honesty is the best policy. For believers, it is far more important to note that honesty is God's policy. And if we are to be servants worthy of our Savior, Jesus Christ, we must be honest and forthright in all our communications with others.

Sometimes, honesty is difficult; sometimes, honesty is painful; sometimes, honesty makes us feel uncomfortable. Despite these temporary feelings of discomfort, we must make honesty the hallmark of all our relationships; otherwise, we invite needless suffering into our own lives and into the lives of those we love.

A Quote to Talk About

There is no secret that can separate you from God's love; there is no secret that can separate you from His blessings; there is no secret that is worth keeping from His grace.

SERITA ANN JAKES

Day 300

TO GOD BE THE GLORY

God is against the proud, but he gives grace to the humble.

1 PETER 5:5 NCV

As Christians, we have a profound reason to be humble: We have been refashioned and saved by Jesus Christ, and that salvation came not because of our own good works but because of God's grace. Thus, we are not "self-made"; we are "God-made" and "Christ-saved." How, then, can we be boastful?

Dietrich Bonhoeffer observed, "It is very easy to overestimate the importance of our own achievements in comparison with what we owe others." In other words, reality breeds humility. So, instead of puffing out your chest and saying, "Look at me!", give credit where credit is due, starting with God. And, rest assured: There is no such thing as a self-made man. All of us are made by God . . . and He deserves the glory, not us.

A Quote to Talk About

Our God is so wonderfully good, and lovely, and blessed in every way that the mere fact of belonging to Him is enough for an untellable fullness of joy!

HANNAH WHITALL SMITH

MISTAKES HAPPEN

Have mercy on me, O God, according to your unfailing love; according to your great compassion blot out my transgressions. Wash away all my iniquity and cleanse me from my sin.

PSALM 51:1-2 NIV

We are imperfect people living in an imperfect world; mistakes are simply part of the price we pay for being here. But, even though mistakes are a part of life's journey, repeated mistakes should not be. When we commit the inevitable blunders of life, we must correct them, learn from them, and pray to God for the wisdom not to repeat them. And then, if we are successful, our mistakes become lessons, and our lives become adventures in growth, not stagnation.

A Quote to Talk About

Mistakes offer the possibility for redemption and a new start in God's kingdom. No matter what you're guilty of, God can restore your innocence.

BARBARA JOHNSON

Day 302

THE GIFT OF THE SHEPHERD

My cup runs over. Surely goodness and mercy shall follow me all the days of my life; and I will dwell in the house of the Lord forever.

PSALM 23:5-6 NKJV

The Word of God is clear: Christ came in order that we might have life abundant and life eternal. Eternal life is the priceless possession of all who invite Christ into their hearts, but God's abundance is optional: He does not force it upon us.

Do you sincerely seek the riches that our Savior offers to those who give themselves to Him? Then follow Him completely and obey Him without reservation. When you do, you will receive the love and the abundance that He has promised. Seek first the salvation that is available through a personal relationship with Jesus Christ, and then claim the joy, the peace, and the spiritual abundance that the Shepherd offers His sheep.

A Talking Point

Today, talk to your daughter about the spiritual abundance that can be hers when she establishes a genuine relationship with Jesus Christ.

WHY DO BAD THINGS HAPPEN?

They won't be afraid of bad news; their hearts are steady because they trust the Lord.

PSALM 112:7 NCV

If God is good, and if He made the world, why do bad things happen? Part of that question is easy to answer, and part of it isn't. Let's get to the easy part first: Sometimes, bad things happen because people disobey God's commandments and invite sadness and heartache into God's beautiful world.

But on other occasions, bad things happen, and it's nobody's fault. So who is to blame? Sometimes, nobody is to blame. Sometimes, things just happen and we simply cannot know why. Thankfully, all our questions will be answered . . . some day. The Bible promises that in heaven, we will understand all the reasons behind God's plans. But until then, we must simply trust that God is good, and that, in the end, He will make things right.

A Talking Point

Today, remind your daughter that it's important to trust God in good times and hard times.

Day 304

PRIORITIES . . . MOMENT BY MOMENT

You can't go wrong when you love others. When you add up everything in the law code, the sum total is love. But make sure that you don't get so absorbed and exhausted in taking care of all your day-by-day obligations that you lose track of the time and doze off, oblivious to God.

ROMANS 13:10-11 MSG

Each waking moment holds the potential to think a creative thought or offer a heartfelt prayer. So even if you're a parent with too many demands and too few hours in which to meet them, don't panic. Be comforted in the knowledge that when you sincerely seek to discover God's priorities for your life, He will provide answers in marvelous and surprising ways.

Remember: this is the day that God has made and that He has filled it with countless opportunities to love, to serve, and to seek His guidance. Seize those opportunities. And as a gift to yourself, to your family, and to the world, slow down and claim the inner peace that is your spiritual birthright: the peace of Jesus Christ.

A Parent Tip

Do first things first, and keep your focus on high-priority tasks. And remember this: your highest priority should be your relationship with God and His Son.

ALWAYS WITH US

For unto us a Child is born, unto us a Son is given; and the government will be upon His shoulder. And His name will be called Wonderful, Counselor, Mighty God, Everlasting Father, Prince of Peace.

ISAIAH 9:6 NKJV

Are you facing difficult circumstances or unwelcome changes? If so, please remember that God is far bigger than any problem you may face. So, instead of worrying about life's inevitable challenges, put your faith in the Father and His only begotten Son: "Jesus Christ is the same yesterday, today, and forever" (Hebrews 13:8 NKJV). It is precisely because your Savior does not change that you can face your challenges with courage for today and hope for tomorrow.

Life is often challenging, but as Christians, we should not be afraid. God loves us, and He will protect us. In times of hardship, He will comfort us; in times of change, He will guide our steps. God is always with us. We must build our lives on the rock that cannot be moved . . . we must trust in God. Always.

A Parent Tip

Examine the patterns in your own life, and understand that you and your children are likely to repeat them. If you don't like the results you've earned from life so far, then change your behaviors.

Day 306

CRITICS BEWARE

Don't pick on people, jump on their failures, criticize their faults—unless, of course, you want the same treatment. Don't condemn those who are down; that hardness can boomerang. Be easy on people; you'll find life a lot easier.

LUKE 6:37 MSG

From experience, we know that it is easier to criticize than to correct. And we know that it is easier to find faults than solutions. Yet the urge to criticize others remains a powerful temptation for most of us. Our task, as obedient believers, is to break the twin habits of negative thinking and critical speech.

Negativity is highly contagious: we give it to others who, in turn, give it back to us. This cycle can be broken by positive thoughts, heartfelt prayers, and encouraging words. As thoughtful servants of a loving God, we can use the transforming power of Christ's love to break the chains of negativity. And we should.

A Parent Tip

Cynicism is contagious, and so is optimism. Raise your children accordingly.

A SACRIFICIAL LOVE

I am the good shepherd. The good shepherd lays down his life for the sheep.

JOHN 10:11 NIV

How much does Christ love us? More than we, as mere mortals, can comprehend. His love is perfect and steadfast. Even though we are fallible and wayward, the Shepherd cares for us still. Even though we have fallen far short of the Father's commandments, Christ loves us with a power and depth that is beyond our understanding. The sacrifice that Jesus made upon the cross was made for each of us, and His love endures to the edge of eternity and beyond.

Christ's love changes everything. When you accept His gift of grace, you are transformed, not only for today, but also for all eternity. If you haven't already done so, accept Jesus Christ as your Savior. He's waiting patiently for you to invite Him into your heart. Please don't make Him wait a single minute longer.

A Parent Tip

Today and every day, give thanks for Christ's sacrifice . . . it is the ultimate expression of His love for you and your family.

Day 308

GOD'S GUIDANCE

Those who are blessed by Him will inherit the land.

PSALM 37:22 HCSB

When we sincerely offer heartfelt prayers to our Heavenly Father, He will give direction and meaning to our lives—but He won't force us to follow Him. To the contrary, God has given us the free will to follow His commandments . . . or not.

When we stray from God's commandments, we invite bitter consequences. But, when we follow His commandments, and when we genuinely and humbly seek His will, He touches our hearts and leads us on the path of His choosing.

Will you trust God to guide your steps? You should. When you entrust your life to Him completely and without reservation, God will give you the strength to meet any challenge, the courage to face any trial, and the wisdom to live in His righteousness and in His peace. So trust Him today and seek His guidance. When you do, your next step will be the right one.

A Talking Point

Today, talk to your daughter about the need to study God's Word and obey it.

CONTENTMENT THROUGH CHRIST

The LORD will give strength to His people; the LORD will bless His people with peace.

PSALM 29:11 NKJV

Everywhere we turn, or so it seems, the world promises us contentment and happiness. But the contentment that the world offers is fleeting and incomplete. Thankfully, the contentment that God offers is all encompassing and everlasting. Happiness, of course, depends less upon our circumstances than upon our thoughts. When we turn our thoughts to God, to His gifts, and to His glorious creation, we experience the joy that God intends for His children.

Do you sincerely want to be a contented Christian? Then set your mind and your heart upon God's love and His grace. Seek first the salvation that is available through a personal relationship with Jesus Christ, and then claim the joy, the contentment, and the spiritual abundance that the Shepherd offers His sheep.

A Parent Tip

Contentment comes, not from your circumstances or your possessions, but from your attitude. And remember this: peace with God is the foundation of a contented life and a contented family.

Day 310

BEYOND GUILT

There is therefore now no condemnation to those who are in Christ Jesus, who do not walk according to the flesh, but according to the Spirit.

ROMANS 8:1 NKJV

All of us have sinned. Sometimes our sins result from our own stubborn rebellion against God's commandments. And sometimes, we are swept up in events that are beyond our abilities to control. Under either set of circumstances, we may experience intense feelings of guilt. But God has an answer for the guilt that we feel. That answer, of course, is His forgiveness. When we confess our wrongdoings and repent from them, we are forgiven by the One who created us.

Are you troubled by feelings of guilt or regret? If so, you must repent from your misdeeds, and you must ask your Heavenly Father for His forgiveness. When you do so, He will forgive you completely and without reservation. Then, you must forgive yourself just as God has forgiven you: thoroughly and unconditionally.

A Parent Tip

Even if you're watching family-friendly programming, television advertisements can be inappropriate for your family. So, at the very least, hit the mute button during all commercials (and make sure your kids do likewise).

ACCEPTING GOD'S GIFTS

For God loved the world in this way: He gave His only Son, so that everyone who believes in Him will not perish but have eternal life.

JOHN 3:16 HCSB

God loves you—His love for you and your family is deeper and more profound than you can imagine. God's love for you is so great that He sent His only Son to this earth to die for your sins and to offer you the priceless gift of eternal life.

You must decide whether or not to accept God's gift. Will you ignore it or embrace it? Will you return it or neglect it? Will you invite Christ to dwell in the center of your heart, or will you relegate Him to a position of lesser importance? The decision is yours, and so are the consequences. So choose wisely . . . and choose today.

A Talking Point

Today, remind your daughter that the appropriate moment to let Jesus rule her heart is always the present moment.

Day 312

FACING LIFE'S TRIALS

Now I take limitations in stride, and with good cheer, these limitations that cut me down to size—abuse, accidents, opposition, bad breaks. I just let Christ take over! And so the weaker I get, the stronger I become.

2 CORINTHIANS 12:10 MSG

Every life (including your daughter's) is a tapestry of events: some grand, some not-so-grand, and some downright disheartening. The Bible promises this: tough times are temporary but God's love is not—God's love lasts forever. Psalm 147 promises, "He heals the brokenhearted and binds up their wounds" (v. 3 HCSB), but Psalm 147 doesn't say that He heals them instantly. Usually, it takes time (and effort) to fix things.

So your daughter should learn that when she faces tough times, she should face them with God by her side. Your daughter should understand that when she encounters setbacks—and she will—she should always ask for God's help. And your daughter should learn to be patient. God will work things out, just as He has promised, but He will do it in His own way and in His own time.

A Parent Tip

All families endure times of sadness or hardship; if your family's troubles seem overwhelming, be willing to seek outside help—starting, of course, with your pastor.

PRACTICAL CHRISTIANITY

If the way you live isn't consistent with what you believe, then it's wrong.

ROMANS 14:23 MSG

As Christians, we must do our best to ensure that our actions are accurate reflections of our beliefs. Our theology must be demonstrated, not only by our words but, more importantly, by our actions. In short, we should be practical believers, quick to act whenever we see an opportunity to serve God.

Are you the kind of practical Christian parent who is willing to dig in and do what needs to be done when it needs to be done? If so, congratulations: God acknowledges your service and blesses it. But if you find yourself more interested in the fine points of theology than in the needs of your neighbors, it's time to rearrange your priorities. God needs believers who are willing to roll up their sleeves and go to work for Him. Count yourself among that number. Theology is a good thing unless it interferes with God's work. And it's up to you to make certain that your theology doesn't.

A Talking Point

Today, remind your daughter that actions always speak louder than words.

Day 314

BEYOND BITTERNESS

Don't insist on getting even; that's not for you to do. "I'll do the judging," says God. "I'll take care of it."

ROMANS 12:19 MSG

Bitterness is a spiritual sickness. It will consume your soul; it is dangerous to your emotional health. It can destroy you if you let it . . . so don't let it! If you are caught up in intense feelings of anger or resentment, you know all too well the destructive power of these emotions. How can you rid yourself of these feelings? First, you must prayerfully ask God to cleanse your heart. Then, you must learn to catch yourself whenever thoughts of bitterness or hatred begin to attack you. Your challenge is this: You must learn to resist negative thoughts before they hijack your emotions.

Matthew 5:22 teaches us that if we judge our brothers and sisters, we, too, will be subject to judgement. Let us refrain, then, from judging our neighbors. Instead, let us forgive them and love them, while leaving their judgement to a far more capable authority: the One who sits on His throne in heaven.

A Parent Tip

Holding a grudge? Drop it! Remember, holding a grudge is like letting somebody live rent-free in your brain . . . so don't do it!

MID-COURSE CORRECTIONS

The sensible see danger and take cover; the foolish keep going and are punished.

PROVERBS 27:12 HCSB

In our fast-paced world, everyday life has become an exercise in managing change. Our circumstances change; our relationships change; our bodies change. We grow older every day, as does our world. Thankfully, God does not change. He is eternal, as are the truths that are found in His Holy Word.

Are you facing one of life's inevitable "mid-course corrections"? If so, you must place your faith, your trust, and your life in the hands of the One who does not change: your Heavenly Father. He is the unmoving rock upon which you must construct this day and every day. When you do, you are secure.

A Parent Tip

Every major change, whether bad or good, puts stress on you and your family. That's why it's sensible to plan things so that you don't invite too many changes into your life at once.

Day 316

OUR CHILDREN, OUR HOPE

Let the little children come to Me; don't stop them, for the kingdom of God belongs to such as these.

MARK 10:14 HCSB

Every child is different, but every child is similar in this respect: he or she is a priceless gift from the Father above. And, with the Father's gift comes immense responsibilities.

Our children are our most precious resource. And, as responsible parents, we must create homes in which the future generation can grow and flourish.

Today, let us pray for our children . . . all of them. Let us pray for children here at home and for children around the world. Every child is God's child. May we, as concerned adults, behave—and pray—accordingly.

A Talking Point

As your daughter grows older, give her age-appropriate responsibilities: Household chores can be wonderful teaching tools. Employ them.

COURAGE DURING TIMES OF CHANGE

Therefore don't worry about tomorrow, because tomorrow will worry about itself. Each day has enough trouble of its own.

MATTHEW 6:34 HCSB

Are you one of those parents who is constantly worried about situations you cannot control? Take your anxieties to God. Are you troubled about changes that threaten to disrupt your life? Take your troubles to Him. Does your corner of the world seem to be trembling beneath your feet? Seek protection from the One who cannot be moved.

The same God who created the universe will protect you if you ask Him . . . so ask Him . . . and then serve Him with willing hands and a trusting heart. And rest assured that the world may change moment by moment, but God's love endures—unfathomable and unchanging—forever.

A Parent Tip

As you face uncertain times, make sure to build your future on a firm foundation: the unshakable foundation of God's eternal promises.

Day 318

CHOOSING WISELY

But the wisdom that comes from heaven is first of all pure; then peace-loving, considerate, submissive, full of mercy and good fruit, impartial and sincere.

JAMES 3:17 NIV

Because we are creatures of free will, we make choices—lots of them. When we make choices that are pleasing to our Heavenly Father, we are blessed. When we make choices that cause us to walk in the footsteps of God's Son, we enjoy the abundance that Christ has promised to those who follow Him. But when we make choices that are displeasing to God, we sow seeds that have the potential to bring forth a bitter harvest.

Today, as you encounter the challenges of everyday living, you will make hundreds of choices. Choose wisely. Make your thoughts and your actions pleasing to God. And remember: every choice that is displeasing to Him is the wrong choice—no exceptions.

A Talking Point

Today, remind your daughter that wise choices bring happiness and unwise choices don't.

HIS INFINITE LOVE

For I am persuaded that neither death nor life, nor angels nor rulers, nor things present, nor things to come, nor powers, nor height, nor depth, nor any other created thing will have the power to separate us from the love of God that is in Christ Jesus our Lord!

ROMANS 8:38-39 HCSB

Christ's love for you is personal. And, His love for your family is personal, too. In fact, He loves you so much that He gave His life in order that you might spend all eternity with Him. Christ loves each of you individually and intimately; His is a love unbounded by time or circumstance.

Are you willing to experience an intimate relationship with Him? Your Savior is waiting patiently; don't make Him wait a single minute longer. Embrace His love today.

A Parent Tip

Through His sacrifice on the cross, Jesus demonstrated His love for you and your child. As a responsible parent, it's up to you to make certain your youngster understands that Christ's love changes everything.

Day 320

THE COST OF IMMORALITY

Let there be no sexual immorality, impurity, or greed among you. Such sins have no place among God's people.

EPHESIANS 5:3 NLT

Your daughter inhabits a society that is filled to the brim with temptations, distractions, and distortions about sex. She is bombarded with images that glamorize sex outside marriage. In fact, she is subjected to daily pressures and problems that were largely unknown to earlier generations. At every corner, or so it seems, she is confronted with the message that premarital sex is a harmless activity, something that should be considered "recreational." But that message is a terrible lie with tragic consequences.

Thankfully, the argument in favor of abstinence isn't a very hard case for parents to make if they're willing to make it. Yet far too many parents are uncomfortable talking to their children about matters pertaining to sex. So they put off those important discussions, sometimes until it's too late. Please don't make that mistake. When the time is right, sit down with your child, have a frank conversation, and make the case for abstinence.

A Talking Point

Today, talk to your daughter about the costs and dangers of immorality.

THE BATTLE IS WON

Cast your burden on the Lord, and He will support you; He will never allow the righteous to be shaken.

PSALM 55:22 HCSB

Christians have every reason to live courageously. After all, the ultimate battle has already been won on the cross at Calvary. But even dedicated followers of Christ may find their courage tested by the inevitable disappointments and fears that visit the lives of believers and non-believers alike.

When you find yourself worried about the challenges of today or the uncertainties of tomorrow, you must ask yourself whether or not you are ready to place your concerns and your life in God's all-powerful, all-knowing, all-loving hands. If the answer to that question is yes—as it should be—then you can draw courage today from the source of strength that never fails: your Heavenly Father.

A Talking Point

Today, talk to your daughter about the rewards of living faithfully, courageously, and obediently.

Day 322

SOLVING LIFE'S RIDDLES

If you need wisdom—if you want to know what God wants you to do—ask him, and he will gladly tell you. He will not resent your asking.

JAMES 1:5 NLT

Life presents each of us with countless questions, conundrums, doubts, and problems. Thankfully, the riddles of everyday living are not too difficult to solve if we look for answers in the right places. When we have questions, we should consult God's Word, we should seek the guidance of the Holy Spirit, and we should trust the counsel of God-fearing friends and family members.

Are you facing a difficult decision? Take your concerns to God and avail yourself of the messages and mentors that He has placed along your path. When you do, God will speak to you in His own way and in His own time, and when He does, you can most certainly trust the answers that He gives.

A Parent Tip

Most parents are sorely tempted to preach to their kids. But what seems like a never-ending river of knowledge (to the parent) sounds like one lecture after another to the child. That's why most parents would be wise to lecture less and listen more.

SENSING HIS PRESENCE

Where can I go from Your Spirit? Or where can I flee from Your presence? If I ascend into heaven, You are there; If I make my bed in hell, behold, You are there. If I take the wings of the morning, and dwell in the uttermost parts of the sea, even there Your hand shall lead me, and Your right hand shall hold me.

PSALM 139:7-10 NKJV

If God is everywhere, why does He sometimes seem so far away? The answer to that question, of course, has nothing to do with God and everything to do with us.

When we begin each day on our knees, in praise and worship to Him, God often seems very near indeed. But, if we ignore God's presence or—worse yet—rebel against it altogether, the world in which we live becomes a spiritual wasteland.

Today, and every day hereafter, thank God and praise Him. He is the Giver of all things good. Wherever you are, whether you are happy or sad, victorious or vanquished, celebrate God's presence. And be comforted. For He is here.

A Talking Point

Today, remind your daughter that God is always present and always available.

Day 324

A ONE-OF-A-KIND TREASURE

Every word of God is pure; He is a shield to those who put their trust in Him.

PROVERBS 30:5 NKJV

God's Word is a roadmap for life here on earth and for life eternal. As Christians, we are called upon to study God's Holy Word, to trust its promises, to follow its commandments, and to share its Good News with the world.

As believers, we must study the Bible and meditate upon its meaning for our lives. Otherwise, we deprive ourselves of a priceless gift from our Creator. God's Holy Word is, indeed, a transforming, life-changing, one-of-a-kind treasure. And, a passing acquaintance with the Good Book is insufficient for Christians who seek to obey God's Word and to understand His will. After all, neither man nor woman should live by bread alone . . .

A Quote to Talk About

Weave the unveiling fabric of God's word through your heart and mind. It will hold strong, even if the rest of life unravels.

GIGI GRAHAM TCHIVIDJIAN

ABUNDANT PEACE

And the peace of God, which surpasses every thought, will guard your hearts and your minds in Christ Jesus.

PHILIPPIANS 4:7 HCSB

Are you the kind of parent who accepts God's spiritual abundance without reservation? If so, you are availing yourself of the peace and the joy that He has promised. Do you sincerely seek the riches that our Savior offers to those who give themselves to Him? Then follow Him. When you do, you will receive the love and the abundance that Jesus offers to those who follow Him.

Seek first the salvation that is available through a personal, passionate relationship with Christ, and then claim the joy, the peace, and the spiritual abundance that the Shepherd offers His sheep.

A Talking Point

Today, talk to your daughter about the difference between material abundance and spiritual abundance.

A TIME TO REST

Come to Me, all you who labor and are heavy laden, and I will give you rest. Take My yoke upon you and learn from Me, for I am gentle and lowly in heart, and you will find rest for your souls. For My yoke is easy and My burden is light.

MATTHEW 11:28-30 NKJV

Sometimes, the struggles of life can drain us of our strength. When we find ourselves tired, discouraged, or worse, there is a source from which we can draw the power needed to recharge our spiritual batteries. That source, of course, is God.

God expects us to work hard, but He also intends for us to rest. When we fail to take the rest that we need, we do a disservice to ourselves and to our families.

Is your spiritual battery running low? Is your energy on the wane? Are your emotions frayed? If so, it's time to turn your thoughts and your prayers to God. And when you're finished, it's time to rest.

A Parent Tip

Do whatever it takes to get enough sleep. Burning the candle at both ends isn't fun or smart. So turn off the TV, and go to bed as soon as possible after your children do. They need a good night's sleep, and so, for that matter, do you.

JOY AND THE CHRISTIAN LIFE

Light shines on those who do right; joy belongs to those who are honest. Rejoice in the Lord, you who do right. Praise his holy name.

PSALM 97:11-12 NCV

Oswald Chambers correctly observed, "Joy is the great note all throughout the Bible." C. S. Lewis echoed that thought when he wrote, "Joy is the serious business of heaven." But, even the most dedicated Christian parents can, on occasion, forget to celebrate each day for what it is: a priceless gift from God.

Today, let us be joyful Christians with smiles on our faces and kind words on our lips. After all, this is God's day, and He has given us clear instructions for its use. We are commanded to rejoice and be glad. So, with no further ado, let the celebration begin.

A Quote to Talk About

As I contemplate all the sacrifices required in order to live a life that is totally focused on Jesus Christ and His eternal kingdom, the joy seeps out of my heart onto my face in a smile of deep satisfaction.

ANNE GRAHAM LOTZ

Day 328

THE WORLD . . . AND YOU

Don't copy the behavior and customs of this world, but let God transform you into a new person by changing the way you think.

ROMANS 12:2 NLT

We live in the world, but we must not worship it. Our duty is to place God first and everything else second. But because we are fallible beings with imperfect faith, placing God in His rightful place is often difficult. In fact, at every turn, or so it seems, we are tempted to do otherwise.

The 21st-century world is a noisy, distracting place filled with countless opportunities to stray from God's will. The world seems to cry, "Worship me with your time, your money, your energy, and your thoughts!" But God commands otherwise: He commands us to worship Him and Him alone; everything else must be secondary.

A Parent Tip

Television is dangerous. So, what should you allow your children to watch on TV? Before you decide which programs are appropriate for your family, ask yourself this question: Does God approve?

THE TREASURE HUNT

For where your treasure is, there your heart will be also.

LUKE 12:34 NKJV

All of humanity is engaged in a colossal, worldwide treasure hunt. Some people seek treasure from earthly sources, treasures such as material wealth or public acclaim; others seek God's treasures by making Him the cornerstone of their lives.

What kind of treasure hunter are you? Are you so caught up in the demands of everyday living that you sometimes allow the search for worldly treasures to become your primary focus? If so, it's time to think long and hard about what you value, and why. All the items on your daily to-do list are not created equal. That's why you must put first things first by placing God in His rightful place: first place. The world's treasures are difficult to find and difficult to keep; God's treasures are ever-present and everlasting. Which treasures, then, will you claim as your own?

A Quote to Talk About

It's sobering to contemplate how much time, effort, sacrifice, compromise, and attention we give to acquiring and increasing our supply of something that is totally insignificant in eternity.

ANNE GRAHAM LOTZ

Day 330

AT PEACE WITH YOUR PURPOSE

But now in Christ Jesus you who formerly were far off have been brought near by the blood of Christ. For He Himself is our peace.

EPHESIANS 2:13-14 NASB

Are you at peace with the direction of your life? If you're a Christian, you should be. Perhaps you seek a new direction or a sense of renewed purpose, but those feelings should never rob you of the genuine peace that can and should be yours through a personal relationship with Jesus.

Have you found the lasting peace that can be yours through Jesus, or are you still rushing after the illusion of "peace and happiness" that our world promises but cannot deliver? Today, as a gift to yourself, to your family, and to your friends, claim the inner peace that is your spiritual birthright: the peace of Jesus Christ.

A Parent Tip

Wise parents know what to overlook. Expect your daughter to be well behaved, but don't expect her to be perfect.

CONSTANT PRAISE

Through Him then, let us continually offer up a sacrifice of praise to God, that is, the fruit of lips that give thanks to His name.

HEBREWS 13:15 NASB

The Bible makes it clear: it pays to praise God. But sometimes, we allow ourselves to become so preoccupied with the demands of daily life that we forget to say "Thank You" to the Giver of all good gifts.

Worship and praise should be a part of everything we do. Otherwise, we quickly lose perspective as we fall prey to the demands of the moment.

Do you sincerely desire to be a worthy servant of the One who has given you eternal love and eternal life? Then praise Him for who He is and for what He has done for you. Praise Him all day long, every day, for as long as you live . . . and then for all eternity.

A Talking Point

Today, talk to your daughter about the importance of praising God now and always.

GOD IS HERE

Draw near to God, and He will draw near to you.

JAMES 4:8 HCSB

God is constantly making Himself available to you and your family; therefore, when you approach Him obediently and sincerely, you will most certainly find Him.

Whenever it seems to you that God is distant, disinterested, or altogether absent, you may rest assured that your feelings are a reflection of your own emotional state, not an indication of God's absence.

If, during life's darker days, you seek to establish a closer relationship with Him, you can do so because God is not just near, He is here.

A Talking Point

Today, talk to your daughter about the need to be still and listen to God.

HONORING GOD

Honor GOD with everything you own; give him the first and the best. Your barns will burst, your wine vats will brim over.

PROVERBS 3:9-10 MSG

Whom will you choose to honor today? If you honor God and place Him at the center of your life, every day is a cause for celebration. But if you fail to honor your Heavenly Father, you're asking for trouble, and lots of it.

At times, your life is probably hectic, demanding, and complicated. When the demands of life leave you rushing from place to place with scarcely a moment to spare, you may fail to pause and thank your Creator for the blessings He has bestowed upon you. But that's a big mistake. So honor God for who He is and for what He has done for you. And don't just honor Him on Sunday morning. Praise Him all day long, every day, for as long as you live . . . and then for all eternity.

A Quote to Talk About

The Holy Spirit testifies of Jesus. So when you are filled with the Holy Spirit you speak about our Lord and really live to His honor.

CORRIE TEN BOOM

Day 334

LIVING IN CHRIST'S LOVE

Yes, my dear children, live in him so that when Christ comes back, we can be without fear and not be ashamed in his presence. If you know that Christ is all that is right, you know that all who do right are God's children.

1 JOHN 2:28-29 NCV

Even though we are imperfect, fallible human beings, even though we have fallen far short of God's commandments, Christ loves us still. His love is perfect and steadfast; it does not waver—it does not change. Our task, as believers, is to accept Christ's love and to encourage others to do likewise.

In today's troubled world, we all need the love and the peace that is found through the Son of God. Thankfully, Christ's love has no limits; it can encircle all of us. And it's up to each of us to ensure that it does.

A Parent Tip

Jesus loves you. His love can—and should—be the cornerstone and the touchstone of your family's life.

HIS POWER AND YOURS

When we were baptized, we were buried with Christ and shared his death. So, just as Christ was raised from the dead by the wonderful power of the Father, we also can live a new life.

ROMANS 6:4 NCV

When you invite Christ to rule over your heart, you avail yourself of His power. And make no mistake about it: You and Christ, working together, can do miraculous things. In fact, miraculous things are exactly what Christ intends for you to do, but He won't force you to do great things on His behalf. The decision to become a full-fledged participant in His power is a decision that you must make for yourself.

In John 14:12, Christ make this promise: "I tell you the truth, whoever believes in me will do the same things that I do" (NCV). So trust the Savior's promise, and expect a miracle in His name.

A Parent Tip

God protects parents and children alike. So if you're feeling a little apprehensive about the future, fear not. God promises to protect every member of your family, and that includes you!

Day 336

FINDING CONTENTMENT

I am able to do all things through Him who strengthens me.

PHILIPPIANS 4:13 HCSB

Where can we find contentment? Is it a result of wealth, or power, or beauty, or fame? Hardly. Genuine contentment is a gift from God to those who trust Him and follow His commandments.

Our modern world seems preoccupied with the search for happiness. We are bombarded with messages telling us that happiness depends upon the acquisition of material possessions. These messages are false. Enduring peace is not the result of our acquisitions; it is a spiritual gift from God to those who obey Him and accept His will.

If we don't find contentment in God, we will never find it anywhere else. But, if we seek Him and obey Him, we will be blessed with an inner peace that is beyond human understanding. When God dwells at the center of our lives, peace and contentment will belong to us just as surely as we belong to God.

A Parent Tip

Contentment comes, not from your circumstances, but from your attitude. And remember this: peace with God is the foundation of a contented life.

DECISION-MAKING 101

Such doubters are thinking two different things at the same time, and they cannot decide about anything they do. They should not think they will receive anything from the Lord.

JAMES 1:8 NCV

From the instant you wake in the morning until the moment you nod off to sleep at night, you have the opportunity to make countless decisions: decisions about the things you do, decisions about the words you speak, and decisions about the thoughts you choose to think.

If you're facing one of life's major decisions, here are some things you can do: 1. Gather as much information as you can. 2. Don't be too impulsive. 3. Rely on the advice of trusted friends and mentors. 4. Pray for guidance. 5. Trust the quiet inner voice of your conscience 6. When the time for action arrives, act. Procrastination is the enemy of progress; don't let it defeat you.

People who can never quite seem to make up their minds usually make themselves miserable. So when in doubt, be decisive. It's the decent way to live.

A Talking Point

Today, remind your daughter that if she's got a decision to make, the first thing she should do is slow down and check it out with God.

Day 338

HAPPINESS AND HOLINESS

Happy are the people who live at your Temple . . . . Happy are those whose strength comes from you.

PSALM 84:4-5 NKJV

Do you seek happiness, abundance, and contentment? If so, here are some things you should do: Love God and His Son; depend upon God for strength; try, to the best of your abilities, to follow God's will; and strive to obey His Holy Word. When you do these things, you'll discover that happiness goes hand-in-hand with righteousness. The happiest people are not those who rebel against God; the happiest people are those who love God and obey His commandments.

What does life have in store for you? A world full of possibilities (of course it's up to you to seize them) and God's promise of abundance (of course it's up to you to accept it). Your Creator has blessed you beyond measure. Honor Him with your prayers, your words, your deeds, and your joy.

A Quote to Talk About

When we do what is right, we have contentment, peace, and happiness.

BEVERLY LAHAYE

LOOKING BEFORE YOU LEAP

An impulsive vow is a trap; later you'll wish you could get out of it.

PROVERBS 20:25 MSG

Are you, at times, just a little bit impulsive? Do you sometimes look before you leap? If so, God wants to have a little chat with you.

God's Word is clear: as believers, we are called to lead lives of discipline, diligence, moderation, and maturity. But the world often tempts us to behave otherwise. Everywhere we turn, or so it seems, we are faced with powerful temptations to behave in undisciplined, ungodly ways.

God's Word instructs us to be disciplined in our thoughts and our actions; God's Word warns us against the dangers of impulsive behavior. As believers in a just God, we should act and react accordingly.

A Talking Point

Today, talk to your daughter about the dangers of impulsive behavior.

THE BREAD OF LIFE

I am the bread of life, Jesus told them. "No one who comes to Me will ever be hungry, and no one who believes in Me will ever be thirsty again."

JOHN 6:35 HCSB

He was the Son of God, but He wore a crown of thorns. He was the Savior of mankind, yet He was put to death on the cross. He offered His healing touch to an unsaved world, and yet the same hands that had healed the sick and raised the dead were pierced with nails.

Jesus Christ, the Son of God, was born into humble circumstances. He walked this earth, not as a ruler of men, but as the Savior of mankind. His crucifixion, a torturous punishment that was intended to end His life and His reign, instead became the pivotal event in the history of all humanity.

Jesus is the bread of life. Accept His grace. Share His love. And follow in His footsteps.

A Quote to Talk About

In your greatest weakness, turn to your greatest strength, Jesus, and hear Him say, "My grace is sufficient for you, for My strength is made perfect in weakness" (2 Corinthians 12:9, NKJV).

LISA WHELCHEL

A PROFOUND LOVE

Go after a life of love as if your life depended on it—because it does. Give yourselves to the gifts God gives you. Most of all, try to proclaim his truth.

1 CORINTHIANS 14:1 MSG

As a parent, you know the profound love that you hold in your heart for your children. As a child of God, you can only imagine the infinite love that your Heavenly Father holds for you. God made you in His own image and gave you salvation through the person of His Son Jesus Christ. And now, precisely because you are a wondrous creation treasured by God, a question presents itself: What will you do in response to the Creator's love? Will you ignore it or embrace it?

When you embrace God's love, your life's purpose is forever changed. When you embrace God's love, you feel differently about yourself, your neighbors, your family, and your world. More importantly, you share God's message—and His love—with others. Your Heavenly Father—a God of infinite love and mercy—is waiting to embrace you with open arms.

A Quote to Talk About

Line by line, moment by moment, special times are etched into our memories in the permanent ink of everlasting love in our relationships.

GLORIA GAITHER

MENTORS THAT MATTER

The lips of the righteous feed many.

PROVERBS 10:21 HCSB

Here's a simple yet effective way to strengthen your faith: Choose role models whose faith in God is strong.

When you emulate godly people, you become a more godly person yourself. That's why you should seek out mentors who, by their words and their presence, make you a better person and a better Christian.

Today, as a gift to yourself, select, from your friends and family members, a mentor whose judgement you trust. Then listen carefully to your mentor's advice and be willing to accept that advice, even if accepting it requires effort, or pain, or both. Consider your mentor to be God's gift to you. Thank God for that gift, and use it for the glory of His kingdom.

A Talking Point

Today, talk to your daughter about the importance of choosing good role models.

A PASSIONATE LIFE

Never be lazy in your work, but serve the Lord enthusiastically.

ROMANS 12:11 NLT

As a thoughtful Christian, you have every reason to be enthusiastic about life, but sometimes the inevitable struggles may cause you to feel decidedly unenthusiastic. If you feel that your enthusiasm is slowly fading away, it's time to slow down, to rest, to count your blessings, and to pray. When you feel worried or weary, you must pray fervently for God to renew your sense of wonderment and excitement.

Life with God is a glorious adventure; revel in it. When you do, God will most certainly smile upon you and your loved ones.

A Quote to Talk About

When the dream of our heart is one that God has planted there, a strange happiness flows into us. At that moment, all of the spiritual resources of the universe are released to help us. Our praying is then at one with the will of God and becomes a channel for the Creator's purposes for us and our world.

CATHERINE MARSHALL

YOUR REAL RICHES

He said, "I came naked from my mother's womb, and I will be stripped of everything when I die. The LORD gave me everything I had, and the LORD has taken it away. Praise the name of the LORD!"

JOB 1:21 NLT

Martin Luther observed, "Many things I have tried to grasp and have lost. That which I have placed in God's hands I still have." How true. Earthly riches are transitory; spiritual riches are not.

In our demanding world, financial security can be a good thing, but spiritual prosperity is profoundly more important. Certainly we all need the basic necessities of life, but once we've acquired those necessities, enough is enough. Why? Because our real riches are not of this world. We are never really rich until we are rich in spirit.

A Talking Point

Today, talk to your daughter about the difference between real riches and earthly riches.

REAL REPENTANCE

I began telling people that they should change their hearts and lives and turn to God and do things to show they really had changed.

ACTS 26:20 NCV

Who among us has sinned? All of us. But the good news is this: When we do ask God's forgiveness and turn our hearts to Him, He forgives us absolutely and completely.

Genuine repentance requires more than simply offering God apologies for our misdeeds. Real repentance may start with feelings of sorrow and remorse, but it ends only when we turn away from the sin that has heretofore distanced us from our Creator. In truth, we offer our most meaningful apologies to God, not with our words, but with our actions. As long as we are still engaged in sin, we may be "repenting," but we have not fully "repented." So, if there is an aspect of your life that is distancing you from your God, ask for His forgiveness, and—just as importantly—stop sinning. Now.

A Quote to Talk About

When true repentance comes, God will not hesitate for a moment to forgive, cast the sins in the sea of forgetfulness, and put the child on the road to restoration.

BETH MOORE

Day 346

A WISE MOVE

But if any of you needs wisdom, you should ask God for it. He is generous and enjoys giving to all people, so he will give you wisdom.

JAMES 1:5 NCV

Do you seek wisdom for yourself and for your family? Of course you do. But, as a thoughtful parent living in a society that is filled with temptations and distractions, you know that it's all too easy for adults and and children alike to stray far from the source of the ultimate wisdom: God's Holy Word.

When you commit yourself to the daily study of God's Word—and when you live according to His commandments—you will become wise . . . in time. So, as a way of understanding God's plan for your life, study His Word and live by it. When you do, you will accumulate a storehouse of wisdom that will enrich your own life and the lives of your family members, your friends, and the world.

A Parent Tip

Simply put, wisdom starts with God. And if you want to convey real wisdom to your daughter, you should study God's Word every day and talk to the Creator often.

FACING UP TO TROUBLE

When you go through deep waters and great trouble, I will be with you. When you go through the rivers of difficulty, you will not drown! When you walk through the fire of oppression, you will not be burned up; the flames will not consume you. For I am the Lord, your God . . . .

ISAIAH 43:2-3 NLT

As life unfolds, all of us encounter occasional setbacks: Those occasional visits from Old Man Trouble are simply a fact of life, and none of us are exempt. When tough times arrive, we may be forced to rearrange our plans and our priorities. But even on our darkest days, we must remember that God's love remains constant.

The fact that we encounter adversity is not nearly so important as the way we choose to deal with it. When tough times arrive, we have a clear choice: we can begin the difficult work of tackling our troubles . . . or not. When we summon the courage to look Old Man Trouble squarely in the eye, an amazing thing usually happens: he blinks.

A Talking Point

Today, remind your daughter that tough times can also be times of intense personal growth.

Day 348

BEYOND ANXIETY

In the multitude of my anxieties within me, Your comforts delight my soul.

PSALM 94:19 NKJV

God calls us to live above and beyond anxiety. God calls us to live by faith, not by fear. He instructs us to trust Him completely, this day and forever. But sometimes, trusting God is difficult, especially when we become caught up in the incessant demands of an anxious world.

When you feel anxious—and you will—return your thoughts to God's love. Then, take your concerns to Him in prayer, and to the best of your ability, leave them there. Whatever "it" is, God is big enough to handle it. Let Him. Now.

A Parent Tip

You know that your daughter is unique and beautiful . . . and you must never become tired of saying so!

KEEPING UP APPEARANCES

We justify our actions by appearances; God examines our motives.

PROVERBS 21:2 MSG

Perhaps you've already discovered that few things in life are more futile than "keeping up appearances," but your daughter may not yet be mature enough to understand the dangers of excessive people-pleasing. After all, the media is trying to convince your daughter that her happiness depends on the color of her hair, or the condition of her wardrobe, or her dress size. But nothing could be further from the truth.

So as you're talking to your daughter, remind her to please God first, not society, not peers, not friends. When she does, she will be blessed today, tomorrow, and forever.

A Talking Point

Today, remind your daughter that if she finds herself focusing too much on her appearance, it's time for her to find a different focus.

Day 350

THE DIRECTION OF YOUR THOUGHTS

My cup runs over. Surely goodness and mercy shall follow me all the days of my life; and I will dwell in the house of the Lord Forever.

PSALM 23:5-6 NKJV

God has given you and your daughter free will, including the ability to influence the direction and the tone of your thoughts. And, here's how God wants you to direct those thoughts: "Finally brothers, whatever is true, whatever is honorable, whatever is just, whatever is pure, whatever is lovely, whatever is commendable—if there is any moral excellence and if there is any praise—dwell on these things" (Philippians 4:8 HCSB).

The quality of your attitude will help determine the quality of your life, so you must guard your thoughts accordingly. If you make up your mind to approach life with a healthy mixture of realism and optimism, you'll be rewarded. So, the next time you find yourself dwelling upon the negative aspects of your life, refocus your attention on things positive. That's the wise way to direct your thoughts.

A Parent Tip

A positive outlook on life is contagious. Your children can catch it from you . . . and they should!

FRIENDS AND FAMILY

As iron sharpens iron, a friend sharpens a friend.

PROVERBS 27:17 NLT

A loving family is a treasure from God; so is a trustworthy friend. If you are a member of a close knit, supportive family, offer a word of thanks to your Creator. And if you have a close circle of trustworthy friends, consider yourself richly blessed.

Today, let us praise God for our family and for our friends. God has placed these people along our paths. Let us love them and care for them. And, let us give thanks to the Father for all the people who enrich our lives. These people are, in a very real sense, gifts from God; we should treat them as such.

A Parent Tip

When your youngster leaves the house, you should know where your child is going, and with whom. And you should also know when your child is expected to return home. That's not being nosy; that's being a concerned parent.

Day 352

THE SHEPHERD'S CARE

Your righteousness reaches heaven, God, You who have done great things; God, who is like You?

PSALM 71:19 HCSB

It's a promise that is made over and over again in the Bible: Whatever "it" is, God can handle it.

Life isn't always easy. Far from it! Sometimes, life can be very, very difficult. But even then, even during our darkest moments, we're protected by a loving Heavenly Father. When we're worried, God can reassure us; when we're sad, God can comfort us. When our hearts are broken, God is not just near, He is here. So we must lift our thoughts and prayers to Him. When we do, He will answer our prayers. Why? Because He is our Shepherd, and He has promised to protect us now and forever.

A Quote to Talk About

When considering the size of your problems, there are two categories that you should never worry about: the problems that are small enough for you to handle, and the ones that aren't too big for God to handle.

MARIE T. FREEMAN

THE GIFT OF GRACE

Saving is all [God's] idea, and all his work. All we do is trust him enough to let him do it. It's God's idea from start to finish! We don't play the major role. If we did, we'd probably go around bragging that we'd done the whole thing! No, we neither make nor save ourselves. God does both the making and the saving.

EPHESIANS 2:8-9 MSG

God has given us so many gifts, but none can compare with the gift of salvation. We have not earned our salvation; it is a gift from God. When we accept Christ into our hearts, we are saved by His grace.

God's grace is the ultimate gift, and we owe to Him the ultimate in thanksgiving. Let us praise the Creator for His priceless gift, and let us share the Good News with all who cross our paths. We return our Father's love by accepting His grace and by sharing His message and His love. When we do, we are eternally blessed . . . and the Father smiles.

A Quote to Talk About

God does amazing works through prayers that seek to extend His grace to others.

SHIRLEY DOBSON

Day 354

THE TRAP OF ADDICTION

Therefore submit to God. Resist the devil and he will flee from you. Draw near to God and He will draw near to you. Cleanse your hands, you sinners; and purify your hearts, you double-minded.

JAMES 4:7-8 NKJV

The dictionary defines addiction as "the compulsive need for a habit-forming substance; the condition of being habitually and compulsively occupied with something." That definition is accurate, but incomplete. For Christians, addiction has an additional meaning: it means compulsively worshipping something other than God.

Your daughter may already know young people who are full-blown addicts, but with God's help she can avoid that fate. To do so, she should learn that addictive substances are, in truth, spiritual and emotional poisons. And she must avoid the temptation to experiment with addictive substances. If she can do these things, she will spare herself a lifetime of headaches and heartaches.

A Talking Point

Today, talk to your daughter about the costs and the dangers of addiction.

LIVING IN AN ANXIOUS WORLD

Cast all your anxiety on him because he cares for you.

1 PETER 5:7 NIV

We live in a world that often breeds anxiety and fear. When we come face-to-face with tough times, we may fall prey to discouragement, doubt, or depression. But our Father in Heaven has other plans. God has promised that we may lead lives of abundance, not anxiety. In fact, His Word instructs us to "be anxious for nothing" (Philippians 4:6). But how can we put our fears to rest? By taking those fears to God and leaving them there.

As you face the challenges of daily life, you may find yourself becoming anxious, troubled, discouraged, or fearful. If so, turn every one of your concerns over to your Heavenly Father. The same God who created the universe will comfort you if you ask Him . . . so ask Him and trust Him. And then watch in amazement as your anxieties melt into the warmth of His loving hands.

A Talking Point

Today, remind your daughter that when she can't sleep, she should talk to the Shepherd.

Day 356

THE FUTILITY OF BLAME

Walking down the street, Jesus saw a man blind from birth. His disciples asked, "Rabbi, who sinned: this man or his parents, causing him to be born blind?" Jesus said, "You're asking the wrong question. You're looking for someone to blame. There is no such cause-effect here. Look instead for what God can do."

JOHN 9:1-3 MSG

To blame others for our own problems is the height of futility. Yet blaming others is a favorite human pastime. Why? Because blaming is much easier than fixing, and criticizing others is so much easier than improving ourselves. So instead of solving our problems legitimately (by doing the work required to solve them) we are inclined to fret, to blame, and to criticize, while doing precious little else. When we do, our problems, quite predictably, remain unsolved.

Have you acquired the bad habit of blaming others for problems that you could or should solve yourself? If so, you are not only disobeying God's Word, you are also wasting your own precious time. So, instead of looking for someone to blame, look for something to fix, and then get busy fixing it.

A Parent Tip

The blame game has no winners. So don't allow your daughter to play it.

DEFEATING DISCOURAGEMENT

The Lord himself will go before you. He will be with you; he will not leave you or forget you. Don't be afraid and don't worry.

DEUTERONOMY 31:8 NCV

When we fail to meet the expectations of others (or, for that matter, the expectations that we have set for ourselves), we may be tempted to abandon hope. Thankfully, on those cloudy days when our strength is sapped and our faith is shaken, there exists a source from which we can draw courage and wisdom. That source is God.

When we seek to form a more intimate and dynamic relationship with our Creator, He renews our spirits and restores our souls. God's promise is made clear in Isaiah 40:31: "But those who wait on the Lord shall renew their strength; they shall mount up with wings like eagles, they shall run and not be weary, they shall walk and not faint" (NKJV). And upon this promise we can—and should—depend.

A Parent Tip

Be a booster, not a cynic. Cynicism is contagious, and so is optimism. Think and act accordingly.

Day 358

LIFE ETERNAL

Because I live, you will live also.

JOHN 14:19 NASB

How marvelous it is that God became a man and walked among us. Had He not chosen to do so, we might feel removed from a distant Creator. But ours is not a distant God. Ours is a God who understands—far better than we ever could—the essence of what it means to be human.

God understands our hopes, our fears, and our temptations. He understands what it means to be angry and what it costs to forgive. He knows the heart, the conscience, and the soul of every person who has ever lived, including you. And God has a plan of salvation that is intended for you. Accept it. Accept God's gift through the person of His Son Christ Jesus, and then rest assured: God walked among us so that you might have eternal life; amazing though it may seem, He did it for you.

A Parent Tip

God offers a priceless gift: the gift of eternal life. Make certain that your daughter understands that the right moment to accept God's gift is always the present one.

EXCELLENCE, NOT EXCUSES

And now, children, stay with Christ. Live deeply in Christ. Then we'll be ready for him when he appears, ready to receive him with open arms, with no cause for red-faced guilt or lame excuses when he arrives.

1 JOHN 2:28-29 MSG

We live in a world where excuses are everywhere. And it's precisely because excuses are so numerous that they are also so ineffective. When we hear the words, "I'm sorry but . . . ," most of us know exactly what is to follow: the excuse.

Because we humans are such creative excuse-makers, all of the really good excuses have already been taken. In fact, the high-quality excuses have been used, re-used, over-used, and ab-used. That's why excuses don't work—we've heard them all before.

So, if you're wasting your time trying to concoct a new and improved excuse, don't bother. It's impossible. A far better strategy is this: do the work. Now. And let your excellent work speak loudly and convincingly for itself.

A Quote to Talk About

Making up a string of excuses is usually harder than doing the work.

MARIE T. FREEMAN

COUNTING YOUR BLESSINGS

Finally brothers, whatever is true, whatever is honorable, whatever is just, whatever is pure, whatever is lovely, whatever is commendable—if there is any moral excellence and if there is any praise—dwell on these things.

PHILIPPIANS 4:8 HCSB

How will you direct your thoughts today? Will you obey the words of Philippians 4:8 by dwelling upon those things that are true and honorable and right? Or will you allow your thoughts to be hijacked by the negativity that seems to dominate our troubled world? Are you so preoccupied with the concerns of this day that you fail to thank God for the promise of eternity? If so, God wants to have a talk with you.

God intends that you experience joy and abundance. So, today and every day hereafter, celebrate the life that God has given you by focusing your thoughts upon those things that are worthy of praise. Count your blessings instead of your hardships. And thank the Giver of all things good for all of the gifts that He has given.

A Parent Tip

It's up to you to live your life—and treat your family—in a way that pleases God because He's watching . . . and so, for that matter, are your kids.

A WALK WITH GOD

I have given you an example to follow. Do as I have done to you.

JOHN 13:15 NLT

Each day, we are confronted with countless opportunities to serve God and to follow in the footsteps of His Son. When we do, our Heavenly Father guides our steps and blesses our endeavors. As citizens of a fast-changing world, we face challenges that sometimes leave us feeling overworked, over-committed, and overwhelmed. But God has different plans for us. He intends that we slow down long enough to praise Him and to glorify His Son. When we do, He lifts our spirits and enriches our lives.

Today provides a glorious opportunity to place yourself in the service of the One who is the Giver of all blessings. May you seek His will, may you trust His Word, and may you walk in the footsteps of His Son.

A Talking Point

Today, talk to your daughter about the need to follow in Christ's footsteps.

ULTIMATE ACCOUNTABILITY

Walk in a manner worthy of the God who calls you into His own kingdom and glory.

1 THESSALONIANS 2:12 NASB

For most of us, it is a daunting thought: one day, perhaps soon, we'll come face-to-face with our Heavenly Father, and we'll be called to account for our actions here on earth. Our personal histories will certainly not be surprising to God; He already knows everything about us. But the full scope of our activities may be surprising to us: some of us will be pleasantly surprised; others will not be.

Today, do whatever you can to ensure that your thoughts and your deeds are pleasing to your Creator. Because you will, at some point in future, be called to account for your actions. And the future may be sooner than you think.

A Talking Point

Today, talk to your daughter about the importance of standing up for her beliefs.

ENTHUSIASTIC DISCIPLESHIP

Don't work hard only when your master is watching and then shirk when he isn't looking; work hard and with gladness all the time, as though working for Christ, doing the will of God with all your hearts.

EPHESIANS 6:6-7 TLB

Jesus has called upon believers of every generation (and that includes you) to follow in His footsteps. And God's Word promises that when you follow in Christ's footsteps, you will learn how to live freely and lightly (Matthew 11:28-30).

Jesus doesn't want you to be a run-of-the-mill, follow-the-crowd kind of person. Jesus wants you to be a "new creation" through Him. And that's exactly what you should want for yourself, too. Jesus deserves your extreme enthusiasm; your family deserves it; and you deserve the experience of sharing it.

A Parent Tip

When it comes to the job of teaching your daughter about Jesus, accountability begins with the person you see in the mirror. As a responsible Christian parent, you should talk about Jesus clearly, confidently, and often.

ABUNDANT LIVING

I came so they can have real and eternal life, more and better life than they ever dreamed of.

JOHN 10:10 MSG

Life is a glorious gift from God. Treat it that way.

This day, like every other, is filled to the brim with opportunities, challenges, and choices. But, no choice that you make is more important than the choice you make concerning God. Today, you will either place Him at the center of your life—or not—and the consequences of that choice have implications that are both temporal and eternal.

We don't intentionally neglect God; we simply allow ourselves to become overwhelmed with the demands of everyday life. And then, without our even realizing it, we gradually drift away from the One we need most. Thankfully, God never drifts away from us. He remains always present, always steadfast, always loving.

As you begin this day, place God and His Son where they belong: in your head, in your prayers, on your lips, and in your heart. And then, with God as your guide and companion, let the journey begin . . .

A Talking Point

Today, talk to your daughter about God's gift of life and the need to treasure that gift.

COMMISSIONED TO WITNESS

Go, therefore, and make disciples of all nations, baptizing them in the name of the Father and of the Son and of the Holy Spirit, teaching them to observe everything I have commanded you. And remember, I am with you always, to the end of the age.

MATTHEW 28:19-20 HCSB

After His resurrection, Jesus addressed His disciples. As recorded in the 28th chapter of Matthew, Christ instructed His followers to share His message with the world. This "Great Commission" applies to Christians of every generation, including our own.

As believers, we are called to share the Good News of Jesus with our families, with our neighbors, and with the world. Christ commanded His disciples to become fishers of men. We must do likewise, and we must do so today. Tomorrow may indeed be too late.

A Quote to Talk About

Our commission is quite specific. We are told to be His witness to all nations. For us, as His disciples, to refuse any part of this commission frustrates the love of Jesus Christ, the Son of God.

CATHERINE MARSHALL

MY FAVORITE VERSES AND IDEAS TO SHARE WITH MY DAUGHTER

Life is too short to spend it being angry, bored, or dull.

BARBARA JOHNSON

MY FAVORITE VERSES AND IDEAS TO SHARE WITH MY DAUGHTER

Character is what you are in the dark.

D. L. MOODY

MY FAVORITE VERSES AND IDEAS TO SHARE WITH MY DAUGHTER

MY FAVORITE VERSES AND IDEAS TO SHARE WITH MY DAUGHTER

By perseverance the snail reached the ark.

C. H. SPURGEON

MY FAVORITE VERSES AND IDEAS TO SHARE WITH MY DAUGHTER

MY FAVORITE VERSES AND IDEAS TO SHARE WITH MY DAUGHTER

Grace grows best in the winter.

C. H. SPURGEON

MY FAVORITE VERSES AND IDEAS TO SHARE WITH MY DAUGHTER

Do noble things, do not
dream them all day long.

CHARLES KINGSLEY

MY FAVORITE VERSES AND IDEAS TO SHARE WITH MY DAUGHTER

MY FAVORITE VERSES AND IDEAS TO SHARE WITH MY DAUGHTER

MY FAVORITE VERSES AND IDEAS TO SHARE WITH MY DAUGHTER

We often become mentally and spiritually barren because we're so busy.

FRANKLIN GRAHAM

MY FAVORITE VERSES AND IDEAS TO SHARE WITH MY DAUGHTER

Life is 10% what happens to you and 90% how you respond to it.

CHARLES SWINDOLL

MY FAVORITE VERSES AND IDEAS TO SHARE WITH MY DAUGHTER

MY FAVORITE VERSES AND IDEAS TO SHARE WITH MY DAUGHTER

In your desire to share the gospel, you may be the only Jesus someone else will ever meet. Be real and be involved with people.

BARBARA JOHNSON